The Eastern Way of Love

TANTRIC SEX AND EROTIC MYSTICISM

Kamala Devi

ILLUSTRATED BY *Peter Schaumann*

SIMON AND SCHUSTER : NEW YORK

PUBLISHED BY SIMON AND SCHUSTER
A DIVISION OF GULF & WESTERN CORPORATION
SIMON & SCHUSTER BUILDING, ROCKEFELLER CENTER
1230 AVENUE OF THE AMERICAS
NEW YORK, NEW YORK 10020

DESIGNED BY IRVING PERKINS
MANUFACTURED IN THE UNITED STATES OF AMERICA

1   2   3   4   5   6   7   8   9   10

LIBRARY OF CONGRESS CATALOGING IN PUBLICATION DATA

DEVI, KAMALA
    THE EASTERN WAY OF LOVE.

    BIBLIOGRAPHY: P.
    1. SEX INSTRUCTION. 2. TANTRISM. I. TITLE.
HQ64.J65   301.41'8   76-50636

ISBN 0-671-22448-4

Contents

Foreword

TO THE AVERAGE WESTERNER, even those who claim sexual liberation and sophistication, sexual activity often lacks the transcending, illuminating, ecstatic heights that storybook romances tell of and movie scores suggest. To most people sexual ecstasy seems an experience that must remain in storybooks, or be the province of a lucky few. As a result, most American sexual activity is simply activity—gymnastic exercise. Because of this, many people seem to experience loneliness, depression and anxiety, even in the midst of a "swinging" sex life. It will come as a surprise and a great adventure to such readers, then, to discover Tantra, an ancient Indian philosophy that teaches, through rituals and exercises, the transforming, wholly integrating experience of Tantric ecstasy.

Tantra works through the body and the mind, in the understanding that if our mental and bodily conditioning rejects sexual pleasure, we can't feel much even if the most accomplished lover is pushing all the recommended buttons.

It is possible through Tantra to have the kind of sexual experience in which one does indeed become one with the universe. The power in this totally experienced sexuality can change lives. It can transform depressed, bitchy, nagging women into sensuous, satisfied, loving people. It can change tired, disappointed, anxious men into recharged, revitalized, exciting human beings. I know. This was my own experience.

Several years ago I became aware of how many of my friends had sexual problems in their marriages. I myself was having great difficulties. After years of marriage, with a kind, loving husband, I felt that I was not really very responsive or interested sexually.

The fact that many women I knew had the same problem did not help my despair.

The trouble in my marriage was ignorance, an unconscious negative attitude toward sex and undeveloped sensuality. There was no place for sexual pleasure in our value system. We never took time to learn about it or explore it. We were on the brink of divorce when a trip to India and into the amazing philosophy of Tantra, saved me, my husband and our marriage. Through Tantra I became a transformed human being. By following the Path of Pleasure, my husband and I reached ecstatic new heights of sexual pleasure. The sexual pleasure was exciting in itself; but ecstasy has an effect on your total self, and that was incredible. Through Tantra we became alive, radiant and joyful human beings.

This book explains my own version of the yoga of sex that I discovered in Calcutta and Kathmandu, adapted for the West from the ancient teachings of the Tantras. It details initiation into the Secret Sex Ritual for a single couple and for a group, and meditations for a psychedelic sex trip (without psychedelics). I have also included exercises for increasing sexual pleasure and a chapter on prolonging sexual ecstasy, almost indefinitely.

I have written this book for my friends, and for all of you I don't know, as a guide to a new freedom and joy in sexuality, and in your life.

1 What Is Tantra? Tantra Is Ecstasy

LONG BEFORE Masters and Johnson, the Tantrics, an elite religious group in the East, were teaching aspects of sexuality that many of us in the West have yet to discover. In Tibet, Nepal, Bengal and South India they taught the Path of Pleasure. They still teach it in secret.

Tantra is a cult of ecstasy, a personal religion based on the mystical experience of joy rather than established dogma. Sex is holy to a Tantric. It is worship; it is energizing and life-giving. Tantric art, writings and religious rituals glorify sex. Tantrics are anti-ascetic; they affirm life. They teach the discovery of the divine through the exhaltation of the total human. They use all of the senses, the mind and the spirit to reach mystic peaks.

Tantrics are affirmatively sexual because they believe that in *maithuna*, or sexual union, man most closely approximates the bliss of union with the divine. According to Orthodox Tantra, a successful maithuna ritual allows a union of the individual self with the cosmic self. The drop, they like to say, becomes one with the ocean. Tantric practice varies from individual to individual, from country to country, from period to period; but each disciple uses meditation and rituals involving all the senses to develop the habit of spiritual bliss.

Tantra must be lived to be fully understood. It promises to enlarge life—to transmute normal human consciousness and energy into the Transcendental Wisdom and the Great Vitality. All this and orgasm, too!

9

Emphasis on the actual personal experience of joy sets Tantra apart from the world's other religions and philosophical systems. Almost all other beliefs teach that to attain a higher reality—be it Plato's ideals or the kingdom of heaven—we must deny our earthly pleasures. We are promised our reward in a better world beyond, which no one has seen. Organized religions establish laws that must be obeyed no matter how they fit our temperaments or circumstances. But a Tantric knows that no man's blood beats in the abstract. Tantric mysticism is based in the concrete.

Mystical experience is foreign to most Westerners. All mystics describe certain elements in common when writing of their experiences, whether they be the Hindu Shankara, the Muslim al-Ghazali, Catholic Saint Teresa, Rufus Jones, a Quaker, or Adam Heshel, a Jew. The mystical state itself is almost beyond expression; and yet anyone who has shared the inward exhilaration will say, "I know."

Tantra teaches that this heightened state, called *samadhi*, is accessible to all serious seekers, and outlines practices and disciplines for attaining it.

Samadhi is a short-lived, passive state in which one feels an absence of will, as if grasped and held by a superior power. The experience is brief; however, the effects are enduring and transfiguring: One strives to be a better person. There is an intellectual awareness of truth beyond normal human understanding, an inkling of eternity. Above all there is a loss of self-consciousness, and a feeling of oneness with God and the cosmos—a cosmic consciousness. Desires are extinguished; the mystic is detached from the chaos of daily events and filled with peace, tranquility and a sense of timelessness.

Most mystics have taught that the seeker must be "purified and delivered from the power of sensual desire" (al-Ghazali).

The psychiatrist and researcher Wilhelm Reich, on the other side, claimed that mystical experience is sublimation or mirror image of the full sexual experience.

Tantrics use sexual power together with proper spiritual preparation to produce a more predictable and intense mystical experience as well as a superlative sexual experience.

Unfortunately, few people know about India's life-affirmative traditions. Today we tend to focus on the country's intense suffering and escapist philosophy. The gurus who teach in the West are usually swamis who are celibate and expect the same of their followers. They withdraw from sensual pleasure because they consider reality a void, the world an illusion, and everyday life a worthless trap.

But doesn't this negation of the senses rob us of the experiences we need for self-knowledge and for survival, to say nothing of joy? India's early Tantrics thought so; they recognized the value of the world they saw, heard and felt. They conditioned themselves physically and mentally to health and happiness.

Instead of reducing things to ciphers and formulas that squash life, Tantra suffuses the most ordinary act with meaning. Breathing becomes glorified as an unrecited mantra or prayer, "Ham sa, Ham sa." The Tantric disciple is taught to think that we are one with the Divine, not in our Final Liberation only, but here and now in every act we do. When this is realized in every natural function, what might have been a mere animal act becomes a religious rite.

This is not the place for an exhaustive philosophical analysis of Tantra. I shall leave that to the sages and merely survey the subject here. It gets complex because Tantric schools exist in both Hinduism and Buddhism. There are minor differences in symbolism and belief; some cults degenerate into magic, even vampirism. (There are even some ascetic Tantrics, but I'm not going to talk about them.) At one time in Tibet Tantric nuns took in young men so the nuns could revitalize their sexually based energies by absorbing their visitors' youthful vibrations (this was usually done indirectly, through a process of meditation, breathing and fantasy called a "subtle embrace"). For all of Tantra's vagaries, however, all its schools cultivate the mystic experience as man's ultimate goal.

No one knows when Tantra began. Hints of its early existence are found in male and female sexual symbols in archeological remains, and in the love poems of India's earliest literature. In one of the Upanishads, written about 1000 B.C., the story of creation begins with God's desire for pleasure. "He was alone; he did not enjoy: One alone does not enjoy: He desired a second and became like a man and woman in close embrace. He made this self of his into two." His desire produced the whole world for him to enjoy.

A Tantric, or *Tantrika* in Sanskrit, is a follower of a series of books called the Tantras. Tantrics consider the most ancient of these books to be part of the Hindu bible, called the Vedas. The earliest are dialogues between the god Shiva and his goddess consort, or Shakti, Parvati.

Being tolerant and undogmatic, Tantrics have borrowed from

the best ideas and practices of their own times and built upon them, carrying both mysticism and erotic practice to new heights. The great Tantraraja Tantra tried to incorporate preexisting Indian beliefs. Because a Tantric is a seeker, he is in harmony with modern science too.

Besides Hindu Tantra, there is also Buddhist Tantra. This was the last form of Buddhism, which began in India and flourished side by side with Hinduism and Jainism. Buddhism at first was concerned only with philosophy and ethics, but in A.D. 100 it split into two factions. The *Hinayana*, or small branch, continued the original ascetic teachings, which did not include a belief in gods. The *Mahayana*, or large branch, incorporated elements from Hinduism and did include the worship of gods and goddesses. It also added the belief in *Bodhisattvas*—beings who selflessly postpone their own salvation to help others. Tantra took its symbolic mythology from this Mahayana branch of Buddhism as well as from Hinduism.

Tantra also borrowed heavily from yoga, adopting the yogic doctrine of union of the individual with the supreme being and the cosmos. To attain the sublime feeling, disciples practiced yogic methods—breath control, exercises, meditation, and chants called mantras—to facilitate mental control.

The Tantric life-style reached its height in India in the eleventh and twelfth centuries. While Europe struggled through the Dark Ages, focusing its thought and art on life after death, India celebrated the joys of this world, especially its sexual joys. India's few remaining Tantric temples display their gods making love in countless positions in the full light of the sun. Worshipers considered this erotica as holy as we do Nôtre Dame de Paris. At this time the Krishna cult, with its emphasis on self-abandonment in love, became incorporated into Tantra.

But Tantra reigned only briefly in India. During most of India's history the Tantrics were forced to worship in secrecy, and they still do.

Tantric beliefs—in a sense, freedoms—conflicted with the practices of Hinduism. Tantra hated the tradition of asceticism which exhorted men to fast, withdraw from women, and mortify the body. In one Tantric myth the goddess makes the point, "My worship is without austerity and pain."

Many Tantric practices, such as the group sex ritual, sex with menstruating women, even eating meat, outraged traditional Hindu mores. The rigid caste system in India held that the shadow of an Untouchable, a member of the lowest caste, was defiling. Yet in their rituals Tantrics often would make love to an Untouchable and call her goddess. These practices were developed in part as shock devices to help individuals break loose from social restraints. One poem illustrates this attempt to shock: "O Goddess Kali, he who on a Tuesday midnight, having uttered your mantra, makes an offering to you in the cremation ground, just once, of a pubic hair from his female partner [Shakti], pulled out by the root, wet with semen poured from his penis into her menstruating vagina, becomes a great poet, and a Lord of the World."*

A young princess spread Tantra to Nepal and Tibet, where it was expressed in the chants of Lamaism and the worship of the doctrine of the Great Delight, represented in the glorious *Yab-Yum* figures. *Yab-Yum* means mother-father. The figures show a god copulating with a goddess as he stands, sits or engages in cosmic dance, which demonstrates the Tantric idea that unity underlies the appearance of duality. The couple is the completed One who is revered, and who symbolize the unity of the cosmos. The Tantrics considered sex a metaphysical mystery in which earthly bliss gives man a taste of the joy of Final Liberation.

This sexual view of the cosmos permeates Tantric art. According to some scholars, the principles of Tantra are the fountainhead of all Indian art.

The Krishna cult inspired some of India's best poetry and miniature paintings. Tantric art, from the powerful bronze Yab-Yum statues to the colorful symbolic paintings that signify the cosmos, can be read on many levels. Colors have meaning: White signifies the nucleus of Being. Red is desire that projects and creates.† The mystic diagrams so often painted, called *yantras*, are phallic symbols.

Sounds also have meanings. The favorite Buddhist mystic phrase, *Om Mani Padme Hum* (Ah, the jewel is in the lotus), has a sexual significance; it indicates that the Bodhisattva has united with his consort. (*Mani* means both jewel and phallic principle. *Padme* means lotus and female sex organ.)

Tantra was ahead of the modern women's liberation movement; the female was recognized as an equal, if different, power.

---

* Rawson, Philip. *Tantra.* London; Arts Council of Great Britain, 1971, p. 9. The Tantrics maintain that a woman's sexual power is at its height during her menstrual period, when her genital tissues are more succulent and engorged than usual and she often feels increased desire. She can use a well-fitting diaphragm to make love without laundry.

† Some authorities, such as Phillip Rawson, say red stands for menstrual blood, white for semen.

Hindu Yab-Yum figures show the goddess, or Shakti, embracing a passive male diety. She represents activity or power; he represents intelligence. Buddhist statues and paintings depict a passive female, wisdom, and an active male, compassion. In both instances Parvati, the female, is no dumb blonde.

In the Tantric rituals for worship, an important component of symbolism illustrates the element of man in woman and woman in man. Many icons in bronze or stone show Shiva as half man and half woman. A new dimension is thus added to the traditional narrow stereotype of sexual identity as each individual realizes his own maleness and femaleness. The aim is to realize that you are complete in yourself, both a man and a woman. You are a god.

Most of the religions of the world conceive of god as a male. Many include phallic worship. Tantra gives equal, often primary, importance to god's female form. Certain sects worship just one goddess, who represents All. "God is one, but men call god many names," starts one Tantric hymn. And the names are like poetry: Shiva, Vishnu, Brahma, Kali, Kamala, Durga, Chitrini, Kundalini, Tara, Sarasvati and so on. Tantric gods may be accepted as reality or as symbols to illustrate psychological truths.

The Tantras teach monism, or the belief that all is one. They call this unifying principle of being *prana*, or energy. They do not split existence into matter and spirit as the dualistic Judeo-Christian tradition does. The Tantrics teach that unity underlies everything. Tantra's basic beliefs are amazingly compatible with twentieth-century science. They developed an atomic theory and bold concepts of space and time, and defined the world as power.

Tantra teaches that the ultimate is present in all living things, whether we call it energy, wisdom, Brahma, Buddha, God or the names of a myriad of gods and goddesses.

Man is taught to look within himself as well as at the world around him for knowledge. This is the Tantric inner vision, summed up in the Vishvasara Tantra: "What is here is elsewhere. What is not here is nowhere." In essence the Tantrics see no separation between body and mind, energy and matter, noumenon and phenomenon, the microcosm and macrocosm.

The Buddhist Tantrics put it this way:

Do not err in this matter of self and other.
Everything is Buddha without exception.
Here is that immaculate and final stage
Where thought is pure in its true nature.

The fair tree of thought that knows no duality
Spreads through the triple world.
It bears the flower of compassion
And its name is service of others.*

Ramakrishna, the nineteenth-century religious teacher, had Tantric leanings. To explain the relationship between the ultimate and its manifestation, he said to think of the sun. "You cannot conceive of the sun's rays without the sun, nor can you conceive of the sun without its rays. . . . One cannot think of the Absolute without the Relative, or of the Relative without the Absolute. . . . The primordial Power is ever at play. She is creating, preserving, and destroying in play, as it were."†

That last line reveals that the Tantrics face the problem of evil and suffering directly. Tantric gods, such as Shiva and Kali, are often shown in their terrible destructive aspects.

In spite of this, Tantra teaches that all of us can cultivate an intense inward vision of joy no matter what the circumstances. And the only garden most of us have to cultivate, certainly the only one we can control, is the interior one.

Tantra is part of the core of incredible optimism that runs throughout Indian thought. The blazing light of ultimate reality is always present like the light of the sun. Although this reality is hidden by clouds of ignorance, man has only to pierce them.

The Tantras tell us to think in these terms: "I am beyond all grief, my true nature is eternal liberation." In many cases this positive attitude kept them from harm. Certain lamas develop their psychic energy so fully they can increase their body heat to enable them to withstand the Tibetan snows.

We can learn much from Tantra's exploration of the suprarational powers of the mind. Tantrics don't reject knowledge that comes from logic, reason or scientific inquiry. But they do go on to explore the realm that exists beyond normal consciousness. "Man's consciousness knows no fixed boundary," they say. *Tan* comes from the Sanskrit root meaning "to expand." We can all expand our horizons, and Tantra tells us how—through meditation, breath control, yoga, art, sex, certain drugs, ritual aids that involve the senses (such as mantras and yantras), loving and a deep commitment to life.

Westerners often misinterpret the Tantric goal of Nirvana.

* de Bary, Wm., ed. *Introduction to Oriental Civilizations: Sources of Indian Tradition.* New York; Columbia University Press, p. 200.

† Zimmer, Heinrich. *Philosophies of India.* Princeton University Press, 1969, p. 564.

Freud was wrong when he called it a death wish. The Tantric Nirvana does not mean obliteration or death, but liberation through wisdom or perfect enlightenment. Nirvana, then, may take place here on earth. It denotes a sorrowless state accessible to all.

Tantrics blow the mind by intensive cultivation of body and mind. The disciple is urged to use the everyday world to find supreme wisdom. He attains Nirvana, or liberation, not by ignoring or deforming his passions, as other forms of Buddhism, Hinduism and almost all world religions teach, but by harnessing, developing and ennobling them. Man must rise through nature, using her, not rejecting her.

The Tantrics cultivate man's sexual energy as a positive force. Modern writers of the Freudian left speak Tantra's language. Wilhelm Reich and Herbert Marcuse, for two, believe that when the life-force—the libido—is repressed, man's latent forces of destruction and death are released. The Tantrics link man's sexuality to the energy of the cosmos. These ancient explorers of experience took the opposite approach from the sexual misers of the world who try to suppress the libido and use the human body as an instrument of labor and production; who try to geld us into docile workhorses.

Tantrics do not want to be cool. They learn to harness and expand their sensual and emotive powers rather than throttle them. The practice of ecstasy becomes an internalized, easily triggered habit. And it begins with the most potent human experience of all, the sexual act. The intensity of this experience can often awaken the most unfeeling, shut-down person.

A Tantric's god or goddess loves him in the flesh. Tantric worship is through the flesh, with body and mind. Tantra says we cannot realize the basic oneness of the universe by will or intellect, but only by experience. In the Panchattattva sex ritual described in the following chapter, carnal knowledge becomes a metaphysical experience of great compassion and oneness. Tantra deals with love, and love means care, care for one's own body as well as all humankind.

This is the Tantric yea to life. "He attains liberation eating the sweet fruits of the world." For me this is Tantra's greatest appeal. The ordinary human life, your path and my path, can become holy simply by attitude.

In Tantra no dogma of sin weighs man down. There is no eternal damnation. Man usually pays the price for his errors here on earth; his redemption is in his own hands. An action is not

good or bad per se but in relation to the whole context, since there are always circumstances in which absolute principles of behavior break down. Therefore: "Whatever harms others is wrong. Whatever harms the doer is wrong. If no one is harmed there is no wrong." Tantra is situation ethics!

Tantra does not pretend to be easy. It has a great respect for the life-force. "This force is like the tension of the bow, which knows not whither the arrow will go," says one of the scriptures. In other words, man can use his life-force well or badly. Morality hinges on two concepts: the duty of compassion, and the need for self-control. The cardinal virtues are discipline, concentration, meditation, resolve, industry, patience, charity, tolerance and joy. But the Tantric path is "as sharp as the edge of a razor, hard to cross and difficult to tread. It is as risky a method as handling a snake, fit only for a hero."

And fit for Americans. The Tantric spirit is fit for people whose lives are not so unbearable as to encourage escape, and who want to live life to its fullest.

2 A Secret Tantra Sex Ritual

SEX AT THE HIGHEST LEVEL is not to be indulged in lightly. The intensity and concentration involved, the focusing of the total human—senses, mind and spirit—make it a tremendously powerful experience. To an Orthodox Tantric this is so because the male and female possess different poles of cosmic bioelectric energy that become united during coitus. This allows the couple to re-energize themselves by absorbing more cosmic energy than they normally do by breathing. Whether we accept this as reality or symbolism, even if we never get to see the sparks fly, a good sexual experience may change us for days, perhaps weeks, perhaps forever. We may awaken with our creative powers enhanced, or remain so preoccupied with the partner that we are unable to work. The effect that our awakened powers have on us will be determined by our ability to put them to use.

A bronze goddess from Kathmandu bursts with energy and desire to touch her god. Her fingers are outstretched touching his, her tongue reaches for her god's mouth, her eyes grip his as he eternally penetrates her body. Her legs encircle his waist and a hand grasps his shoulder. He stands on one leg in cosmic dance, one arm holding her waist. Both faces radiate supreme joy.

This icon shows how Tantrics worship at the highest level of practice; sometimes standing, sometimes sitting, most often lying together deeply locked in a complete sexual embrace.

A Tantric sex ritual for worship is the best living example of the Path of Pleasure. Experiencing this form of worship can add to our spiritual life as well as our sex life. Although I have explained some of the ideas of Tantra to you, it is important to comprehend how much of success in understanding Tantra—

really *understanding*, in your body as well as your mind—depends on your attitude. If you approach the following ritual in an attitude of worship, chanting foreign words and phrases may not seem embarrassing. If it does, omit the Indian expressions and use your own private words of love and endearment. Do not proceed with this ritual if you feel self-conscious. You must focus on letting yourself be freed. If you feel hesitant, read on and do not attempt the ritual until later.

This is the Panchattattva, a Bengali ritual which I have adapted to suit Western needs. Elements vary in the teachings of different gurus and in different parts of the Tantric world—India, Nepal or Tibet.

The first consideration is the selection of the ceremonial sex partner, the Shakti (female) or Shakta (male). The partner can be a wife, a husband, or someone who is ritually married only for the purpose of this sexual union (called a Shiva marriage). During the sacramental union the man incarnates the god Shiva and the woman incarnates the goddess Parvati. The choice of partners is not to be made lightly: choose someone you admire and find exciting.

The best time for the sacrament is said to be from 7 P.M. to midnight, although the sacrament may be taken at any time convenient.

The Tantras advise that the ceremony must never be entered into in total darkness. The room should be clean, pleasing and airy. The temperature should be adjusted so as to enable the couple to remain comfortably naked for at least an hour. Mirrors enable you to see the beautiful movements of your bodies. Use them if possible. Fur on the bed in winter and satin in summer enhance the situation, and if you have fresh flowers available, add them.

A number of symbolic articles should be laid out on an elegant cloth before the rite begins. These include:

A dish or tray containing small amounts of freshly cooked meat, fish, bread, or cooked rice. The Bengalis like to use whole cardamom seeds, but these may be difficult to obtain.

Two glasses and a pitcher of fresh, cold drinking water.

A decanter of wine, or any favorite alcoholic beverage.

Two candles in holders.

Essence of musk, incense, or any good perfume.

Each article has a symbolic meaning. According to the scriptures, they represent, along with sexual intercourse, the entire universe.

Wine, according to one of the Tantras, represents fire. It signifies creative cosmic energy that brings joy to man and banishes his sorrows. It loosens man's inhibitions and brings him closer to the radiant core.

Meat represents all animal life. It reminds man of his origin in nature.

Fish represents sea life.

Cereal symbolizes the earth.

The last and most important element in the worship is sexual union itself, which represents cosmic energy, the very root of the world.

The couple may bathe before arriving, but I think it preferable for them to bathe each other gently and thoroughly. Soap each other carefully, then rinse and dry each part of the body, giving special attention to the feet, the genitals and the pubic hair. Open the vulva. Pull back the foreskin if there has been no circumcision. Make sure everything is clean.

After the bath, massage each other with perfumed oil. Purists like to use a different scent for each part of the body but I prefer to use just one, with a musk base. This should never be changed so that in future unions the power of conditioning and reinforcement can conjure up past pleasure. Massage the nape of the neck, the arms, the breasts, the belly, the thighs and the feet. Be careful to avoid the erogenous zones; the perfume may burn the tender skin. In subsequent rituals the smell alone should be enough to set currents of desire flowing.

The Shakti should then put on a red robe, preferably the shade of hibiscus, the symbolic flower of Tantra. The male wears a garment made of a natural fabric of any color.

An Orthodox Tantric would perform preliminary yogic disciplines such as chants and exercises but the only ones recommended for the Westerner are the breathing exercises (discussed in Chapter 3) to dispel tension and anxiety.

Once your breathing is regular and deep, hold your breath for seven seconds and concentrate on the Muladhara chakra, or sex center, located between the anus and the genitals. Here sleeps Kundalini, a serpentine form of energy, visualized as a snake sleeping with her tail in her mouth. Ecstasy occurs when she rises completely to unite with Shiva, who is located in your head. Contract the sphincter muscles of the anus to stimulate the sex chakra.

Now contemplate the creative union that takes place between the two cosmic elements, consciousness and energy, which are represented by the god Shiva and the goddess Parvati. When this union occurs, a vital current will flow upward through your spine to the top of your head. If you can't feel it right away, then imagine it!

Hold your breath and visualize sexual intercourse in your favorite position—step by step from the very first touch.

Pour two small glasses of wine. Then lift your glasses and drink together.

Again fill the glasses, one-third full. Now take a piece of meat and repeat the names of the gods, Shiva and Parvati, several times. If you can keep in mind that you represent gods, use your own given names. Eat the meat and finish your wine.

Again partly refill the glasses with wine and eat a small piece of fish. Then have the cereal and finish with more wine.

At this point you should meditate on the Kundalini. Think of it as divine consciousness in your body, which later will let you not only know but feel that matter is energy.

Now rinse your mouths with water and eat the cardamom seed to sweeten your breath, after first meditating on how the outer husk of the seed hides the two halves of the kernel. The Tantras say that all creation is also a unity that only appears to be a duality.

You are now ready to go to the bed.

The man unveils his Shakti and seats her while he stands in front of her. He arranges the light so that it falls on her naked body.

He thinks of her as a goddess and tells her so. She is the mystery of creation and the secret of life. "She is the awakener of pure knowledge and the embodiment of all bliss." Unless the worshiper can conceive of his partner in these terms it is useless to go on with the maithuna, for it will be no different from ordinary intercourse.

To identify yourselves with the cosmic union of Shiva and his consort, both of you say in Bengali, *Shiva hum, So' hum.* This means "I am Shiva, I am she." If you feel uncomfortable saying this, say each other's names.

The male now places his fingertips on the Shakti's body to awaken the dormant forces there. He should touch her heart, the crown of her head, her eyes (and a symbolic eye in the center of her forehead), the hollow of her throat and her earlobes. He then touches her nipples twice, moving in a circular motion around the outside of the aureola. He moves to her navel, tracing a circle around it lightly, then to her thighs, knees, feet and

genitals. Here he may open the petal lips of the vulva (the *yoni*) and observe the deepening color of its inner parts. If he uses his tongue he can increase the power of awakening.

Then the man may take ashes or red Kum-Kum powder* to mark her body in several places. He uses the first three fingers of each hand to draw three parallel lines (the *Tripura*) as shown in many Tantric paintings. He marks the forehead, breasts, waistline, abdomen, upper arm, elbow and wrists.

The Shakti then performs the same procedure on the man. She kneels at his feet and worships him as the Lord Shiva. She marks his body and may choose to touch his sensitive parts with her lips; especially the head of his penis. The Tantras describe the awakening in these terms: "As Kundalini ascends she pierces each petal, which then rises up erect as she passes."†

Now lie side by side on the bed, breathing regularly and deeply, joining the rhythms of your breath without touching. The deep relaxed breathing helps to spread your growing excitement to the whole body rather than just the genitals.

A number of maithuna positions are shown in Tantric paintings and sculpture; a favorite has the woman on top. For many people the most comfortable position is on the side, so I recommend this for your first ritual. Once yoga has strengthened your back you may prefer a sitting posture.

Keep as much contact as possible between the two bodies: nipples and breasts together, eyes locked; faces close enough to inhale each other's breath; hands and fingers interlaced in total communion.

Now, remaining fully relaxed, the male parts the labia of the *yoni* and inserts his *lingam* (penis). The jewel is now in the lotus—a reference to the Buddhist mantra, *Om Mani Padme Hum.*

This begins the holy sexual union.

The man should not move or thrust, but just fill the woman with his hard virility as he grasps her buttocks and pushes deep inside her to the root of his sex. The Shakti may gasp at the electric touch of him and moan as she feels her yoni respond and become heavy and tight with sensation as it envelops him. As her vagina begins to stir and grip the male's lingam a deepening pleasure will permeate and seize her whole body and his. The

* Any red powder will do.
† Marqués-Rivière, Jean. *Tantrik Yoga: Hindu and Tibetan.* London; Rider, and Co., 1940, p. 64.

yoni will contract, opening and closing to seek more pleasure like a mouth quietly sucking. The man should feel that he is possessing the woman and is being possessed by her at the same time.

The man may withdraw a bit, as if to make room for the pressing contractions that lure him back into the depths of her.

Keep looking into the partner's face to see the mounting pleasure written there.

In Bengal the pair would not talk or laugh. The quietness helps them to feel every movement and ripple of her warm flesh around his sex.

There should be a complete absence of striving and tension. All movement is interior. The throbbing lingam is deep inside the grasping, caressing, loving yoni as the woman moves inside her depths. Lie together like this for perhaps thirty minutes and visualize the flow of current and love between you. A feeling of heat will rise and be most intense where the genitals meet, as if they were being fused.

Meditate upon the miracle that is about to take place. Cast out all anxieties and forget yourself. Let go. Let go. Let go.

If the maithuna is successful, the muscles of both bodies should contract involuntarily. Searing currents of pleasure should shoot everywhere—down the legs until they tickle the soles of the feet, up into the arms and fingers, touching the buttocks, and flicking past the nipples and up into the brain.

A sudden peak of ecstasy steals upon you. The moment comes like a thunderbolt. A shuddering flash pierced by awareness should seize you in a moment filled with overpowering brilliance, like a point in which all lesser moments of life are focused.

Tantrics describe this blinding moment as the union of the risen Kundalini, or sexual energy, which shoots up to join with Shiva, or the psyche. Many yogis speak of having perceived great light—a light so bright it bears no relation to visible light, yet so intimate, so profound, so vast it neutralizes every lesser experience.

The moment is beyond the senses, as if there has been an immediate and profound contact with the truth. There is no voice, no image, no vision—only cosmic presence. You cut through the barriers of time and place like a laser, to know eternity. There is no distinction between knower, knowledge and the object of knowledge. You are absorbed in the truth, a truth above concepts, above all understanding. Truth that belongs to the order of knowledge, yet more to the order of love.

You feel that you, your partner and the world are all one beat of the same pulse. There is no other.

The self is annihilated so that you become pure capacity for the divine. You are opened up into an immensity of liberty and exultation, bursting into a realm of splendor that glows with indefinable fire. You enter in serene confidence into heights that leave one inarticulate, feeling the throb of the universal.

Love floods out as if new fountains of spiritual energy have been opened. There is a sense of community with the pulsating cosmos.

The breathless, vibrating peak of joy is followed by a feeling of the emptying of the self. All pent-up tension drains out and you experience the peace of samadhi. There is nothing that can disturb the heart of that peace. You have been stripped naked to the literal substance of the self, the irreducible ground of being. You have surrendered the ego to find it at a higher, stronger level.

Afterward there is complete release, rest—as if you have finally arrived at the destination. Your life has been shot through with eternity. Yearning has become consummation in timeless intensity. You have opened a door no man can shut.

Keep the genitals together, the lingam touching the yoni, as long as possible to enjoy the quiet exchange of heat and energy that continues to give pleasure. You may not be able to tell where one body ends and the other begins, whether it is her hair or your hair, his skin or your skin.

If the ritual is successful you will have perceived the realm of Great Bliss. You should return in radiance from contact with your Diamond Being, or essence. You should feel immaculate and conscious of your intrinsic purity.

If this feeling of being cleansed and revitalized is not present, the ritual has failed. But be patient and try again.

Maithuna's psychic fruits are wisdom and liberation. During this ceremony the individual transcends time and death to share a feeling of eternity. Your mind is no longer bound by logic and reason. Knowledge becomes spontaneous and intuitive. Your experience is what the Greeks call *ek-stasis*. After maithuna, many yogis speak of being possessed by a deep passion to have their lives become radiation centers of love. The experience contributes to self-integration, stability and maturity. By losing yourself, you find a stronger, deeper self. A sense of center remains, where you can live.

Remember that the rite cannot be undertaken in a spirit of duty or greed. Mystical ecstasy cannot be wrung from sex or worship in a spirit of taking. It is found by waiting, opening up and letting go.

3 Yoga Exercises for Increasing Sexual Pleasure

EVEN A MINIMAL KNOWLEDGE of yoga, especially the techniques of regular breathing and relaxation, is a great boon to anyone. Yoga can bring peace and serenity to those, like me, who suffer from a shaky-hand syndrome when we are under pressure and all wound up. And the practice of yoga exercises can bring a new capacity for sexual enjoyment. Relaxing with yoga fights anxiety, the great enemy of sex, which has become a fact of life in the modern world.

Yoga is far more than another set of setting-up exercises. It is a 2000-year-old Hindu philosophy, with the goal of complete self-realization for the individual. Yoga has influenced the Tantrics, the Ceylonese, Tibetans, Taoists, followers of Zen and other Buddhists, as well as modern students of natural child-birth, mind control and autogenic training.

Yoga teaches that the key to health, happiness and mental calm lies within. The Sanskrit root of the word has two meanings: first, to meditate or go into a trance; second, to yoke to a higher nature within us all. The goal is to awaken a new transcendental self which will enhance our wisdom and vitality as well as our powers of love and ecstasy.

Although the common stereotype of a yogi is an ascetic, Tantric yoga is sensual, as you know from reading the ritual. But eventually yoga lets us go beyond the world that is measured through our senses. By teaching control of both the body and the mind, it lets us go beyond their limitations to get in contact with our subconscious, develop our extrasensory perception, and learn to transcend time and space in our understanding.

There are a number of schools and sub-schools of yoga, but all start with the basic breathing exercises. These techniques bring an optimum amount of oxygen to the lungs and increase circulation. The steady rhythm of deep breathing helps to keep fear and anxiety from constricting us. Wilhelm Reich observed that neurotics do not breathe properly. They draw quick, shallow breaths with an irregular rhythm, like an excited dog panting. Statistically, they suffer from far more respiratory trouble than other people. Deep breathing does not mean sucking in a huge breath and puffing out the upper chest like a pigeon. It involves rhythmically filling and emptying the lower part of the lungs reaching to the diaphragm, as well as the upper part of the lungs. When you watch a yogi breathing deeply his chest does not heave, but you can see his upper abdomen rise and fall as he fills and empties his lungs.

Teachers of yoga talk of maintaining proper contact with prana, conceived as the vibratory aspect of universal energy. In perfect health there is a balance of prana in your body, so mental and physical health are based on the proper management of the body's electricity. This is why yogis pay so much attention to the art of breathing: breathing is more than just a matter of absorbing oxygen and exhaling carbon dioxide; we inhale pranic vibrations too when we breathe. Yogic breathing and postures, and also the maithuna sex ritual, can help to re-energize the body by increasing the absorption of prana to keep vitality at its peak.

D. H. Lawrence understood the Tantric vision of energy and presented it exquisitely. He saw it as a life-force capable of being sucked out of a man, or, by the power of sexual love, fanned into a fierce living flame. This undulating, serpentine energy is present in all living things. Wilhelm Reich called it the orgone.

Kundalini is a form of this energy; this world serpent, shown swallowing her tail, is usually lying quiescent behind your genitals, but you can learn to awaken her by the sex ritual, as described in the previous chapter.

Such a world view implies tremendous personal responsibility for our health, our emotions, our thoughts, our opinions, our passions. Since our responses and our actions are basically in our power, we must act to fashion ourselves in a Godly image, not only potent but compassionate.

Yoga was developed in special ways by the Tantric schools of the Middle Ages, which adopted much of royal yoga (raja yoga),

the yoga of force (hatha yoga), the yoga of spells (mantra yoga), and the yoga of dissolution (laya yoga) for their own purposes. The course of training includes: self-control according to the moral rules (*yama*); posture (*asana*); control of the breath (*pranayama*); restraint (*pratyahara*), in which the sense organs are trained to take no note of their perceptions so as to not interrupt the tranquil mind with their messages; steadying the mind (*dharana*) by concentrating on one thing, such as an icon, a concept or a sacred symbol; meditation (*dhyana*); and the mystical state (*samadhi*) in which the whole personality is temporarily dissolved.

Although their aims and results are similar, Tantric yoga is much easier to practice than Zen, and is more sure to bring fruit. Unlike Zen, which outlines no steps, no path to follow, and expects you to take a massive leap to spontaneous insights after twenty years of trying, yoga gives you tools and a map for each step.

An exhaustive study of any one of these schools can, with a guru, take a lifetime, as is often the case among Tibetan monks, who may repeat certain mantras 100,000 times during a two-year period if they are diligent. Yet benefits from the principles and practices are accessible to anyone with the desire to learn and a few minutes of regular practice to enrich his own life.

Yoga involves both internal and external practice done together; but to simplify learning, I shall separate the two and start with some of the external practices, such as breathing, relaxation and exercises.

On the first level of basic health, yogis have long known that the mind can be used to exert control over the body, and that certain processes which we call autonomic and believe to be beyond our conscious control can be modified. These include blood pressure, heart rate and metabolism. The increasing interest of Western doctors in yoga, breathing and biofeedback show the mounting importance of these ideas in the West.*

Many millions of Americans suffer from stress-produced illnesses; thirty-three million suffer from hypertension, or high blood pressure, alone. Stress and anxiety in the modern world often overstimulate the body's "fight-or-flight" mechanism with an extra dose of adrenaline, causing the heart to beat faster, muscles and blood vessels to contract, digestion to be suspended. Such a response is often necessary for survival on the savannah

* *Biofeedback and Self Control.* Theodore X. Barber, *et al.* Chicago & New York; Aldine, 1971.

or in the jungle, but it can be deadly if prolonged and made into a habit. As stressful situations increase in daily life, when simply getting to work can make us frightened or angry, when we drive ourselves at double time living by the clock, then this fight-or-flight state may become habitual. Our body regulators of glands, particularly the hypothalamus, and hormones may become set at too high a level, like a thermostat, driving us, and especially our hearts, at a fast pace, often producing a number of stress-related ills. These include impotency, for a man on amphetamines or in a hyperactive state usually finds it difficult or impossible to have an erection.

The great benefit of yogic techniques for breathing, relaxation and meditation is that they induce changes in the autonomic balance by setting the body's thermostat, the hypothalamus, at a lower level—much as a motor that idles too fast, burning too much fuel and straining the mechanism, can be reset. You can learn to lower your metabolism, including blood pressure, putting yourself back in idle, if you will. These simple techniques can save lives, as the reports of doctors working with autogenic therapy will substantiate. Reports in *Biofeedback and Self Control* support the claims of yogis that many of the processes we consider automatic are subject to a certain amount of modification under our control. In just twenty minutes, practiced students of yoga and meditation slow their metabolism, lower their blood pressure, decrease oxygen consumption, and reduce the work of their hearts by thirty percent, as if they had experienced a state of rest equal to the deepest sleep. Below are some yoga exercises I think everyone will find helpful.

SHAVASAN   Shavasan is a yoga exercise for relaxation, useful as a preliminary to the sexual positions.

Have a light meal an hour or so before the exercise. Wear light, loose clothing.

Lie down with lower limbs apart and arms at a 15 degree angle from the body, fingers semi-flexed. Close your eyes and feel the eyelids droop. Turn your eyeballs upward as if you were looking at your brows through your eyelids.

Breathe slowly, rhythmically and deeply, filling and emptying the whole of your lungs. Your abdomen should rise when you inhale. Once you establish a slow, even rhythm, concentrate on the sensation at your nostrils. Feel the coolness of the inspired air and the warmth of the expired air. This should foster relaxation by helping you to become inwardly alert, forgetting both the environment and any preoccupations.

Relax your muscles so that you feel heaviness in different parts of your body, starting with the extremities. First relax your feet, which should droop; then your ankles and your knees, working up to your trunk, head and face. Try lifting a hand and letting it flop, flaccid, to make sure it is relaxed. Finally, relax your eyes and mouth; let your jaw sag with teeth unclenched.

Stop the spontaneous activity of your mind, think of the void, fill your mind with peace. Unplug your sense organs and "one-point the mind," as yogis like to say.

Most people learn the exercise in about three weeks. Try to do it for thirty minutes in the beginning if you can; but as little as three to five minutes can be good for you, especially before going to bed for the night.

Doctors have found that patients with high blood pressure show a reduction in symptoms after doing this simple exercise daily for a few weeks. Insomnia, headaches, nervousness, irritability and giddiness disappeared in almost all patients.

Shavasan is a good exercise to avoid hypertension and anxiety; it brings on relaxation and can aid in the attainment of sleep or a sexual motive state. The exercise usually brings a sense of well-being as well.

SALUTE TO THE SUN AND EARTH

My favorite yoga exercise—besides the maithuna positions, of course—is what I like to call "salute to the sun and earth."

Begin by standing comfortably erect, feet slightly apart. Rise on your toes, reaching up toward the sun first with one hand and then the other. Stretch the top of your head as high as it will go and make your neck as long as possible. Continue until you feel a tingling in your fingertips. Then let your body fall forward from the waist, folding toward the floor. Relax completely so that your head and fingertips feel heavy. Repeat this any number of times.

If possible, I highly recommend studying yoga more deeply. The Cobra, the Bow, the Lotus, the Tree, the Curling Leaf, the Fish, the Little Bird (open your thighs wide and stretch out your modesty muscles), and the rest are all exercises of great benefit—if you stay away from the ascetics. Learning to relax the body helps to relax the mind and character armor, an ancient idea of interdependence reaffirmed by Reichian therapy. Learning physical and mental control is vital in the modern world, and if we can't relax we can't feel pleasure fully.

PRANAYAMA   The yogic system of deep breathing is slow, rhythmical, and involves the abdomen and diaphragm as well as the upper and lower chest in one unbroken, continuous process. Many people repress their breathing to repress feelings, so diaphragmatic breathing may bring out deep feelings.

Theory has it that deep breathing prevents passivity in the respiratory system, first by drawing in larger quantities of air, containing oxygen and prana, and secondly, by using that air to energize important spinal nerve centers. Symbolically, Tantrics speak of five or six of these nerve centers, which they call *chakras*, or lotus centers, including the Muladhara sex center already mentioned, a heart center, and the thousand-petaled Shiva center in the head.

The best conditions for practice are in the open air, on an empty stomach, both morning and evening, concentrating on the glowing center between your eyes (the Ajna chakra). Maintain a rhythm of inhalation and exhalation, counting to six or seven, retaining for the count of one or two according to your lung strength. While practicing, keep the mental feeling that all bodily impurities and mental disturbances are going away with each exhalation and that positive thoughts and vibrations are entering with each inhalation. You should feel your energy and potency growing.

People who begin with weak and neglected lungs should start by concentrating on exhalation only, since if you exhale fully you will inhale automatically. After practicing exhaling to the utmost, inhale slowly from the abdomen as much air as is comfortable. Gradually increase the intake until the upper part of your lungs is also being filled. Avoid jerks, and practice breathing rhythmically, for one secret of the exercise is tuning in to the fundamental rhythms of the universe and feeling at one with nature.

There are a number of simple and beneficial pranayams, or breathing exercises, for revitalizing your entire system, including:

1. *Nadi Shodan* (nerve cleaning). Sit erect in some easy posture, as relaxed as you can. Close your eyes and inhale slowly through the left nostril, keeping the right one closed with your

thumb. Breathe in as deeply as possible without forcing; then exhale through the right nostril, without retaining the breath, slowly and gradually in one stream. Repeat, this time inhaling through the right nostril and exhaling from the left. This is one pranayam. Practicing this for several minutes a day will increase your lung strength. Concentrating on the Ajna chakra between your eyebrows and summoning a joyful mental attitude will enhance the effect of this pranayam.

2. *Anulom-vilom.* Sit in an easy posture. Exhale quickly through the left nostril, stopping the right one with the thumb. Then inhale quickly through the left nostril and exhale with some force from the right nostril. Do this fifteen to twenty times, alternating nostrils, as you meditate on the Clear Light. This is especially good for clearing the nose if you have a cold.

3. *Sukh Purvak.* Sit on the bed or floor, legs crossed in the lotus position (*padmasana*) or tailor fashion. Close your right nostril with your right thumb and inhale very slowly through your left nostril. Then close the left nostril with the ring finger of your right hand. Retain the air as long as is comfortable, and then exhale very, very slowly through your right nostril. Complete the process in a similar way by inhaling from the right nostril and exhaling from the left nostril, after retaining the air for several seconds without causing strain or discomfort. To start with, three to five of such pranayams will do. Then gradually increase the number to twenty each time, both morning and evening, if possible.

Repeat a long-drawn-out mantra such as OM at the beginning of each session, until you can feel vibrations in your air passages. This helps to loosen tense muscles in your head and neck, which sometimes cause headaches. This is the way I ward off a tension headache if I feel one coming on.

BHASTRIKA, OR BREATH-OF-FIRE   Sit erect in the lotus position, the padmasana, or some other stable, comfortable posture. Inhale and exhale quickly, panting hard and producing a hissing sound, for about twenty breaths at first. Once you are used to the Breath-of-Fire you may want to continue this up to two minutes before resting, but work up gradually, because students sometimes feel dizzy or giddy at the start. Follow the fast breathing by a very deep inhalation, suspension of breath for a comfortable limit, and then slow, deep exhalation. Continue again for at least three rounds.

When I sit in one of the yoga postures and do the Breath-of-Fire for two minutes, then relax and breathe deeply, holding this breath before exhaling, I can produce a high similar to marijuana, where my chest seems to expand and my body feels lighter. This seems to lighten all my burdens and make me feel more integrated. Try experimenting with the timing of the Breath-of-Fire to become a sky flier without any need for drugs.

When done in the morning standing in front of an open window and quickly moving your arms, stretched out at your sides, ten inches forward and ten inches back, the Breath-of-Fire is a good way to overcome sluggishness and depression and get yourself going, free of preoccupations and anxieties.

4 Meditation: Dhyana

THE BEARDED, long-haired yogi in loose white Indian dress sits in the lotus position in front of his open window in Kashmir, looking straight ahead, spine upright and head erect. He sits motionless for nearly an hour, until the sun rises. No outward sign betrays the inner transformations he describes later.

The clean-cut American businessman sits at his desk with his hands folded in his lap. His eyes are closed and he does not move for twenty minutes. Then he stands up, collects his papers, and leaves for an important meeting.

Both men are exploring the infinite interior frontier that lies at everyone's disposal. Both are using meditation to enrich their lives at different levels: the businessman for improved health, relaxation and a sense of well-being; the yogi for a measureless mystical experience. Meditation and its complement, visualization, can also help to overcome sex problems and make a good sex life even better.

Many Westerners, including busy executives, have found that they benefit from the stillness of meditation to quiet their minds from the whirlwind of everyday concerns. Meditation can help them to change direction, perhaps find new ideas and practical answers to problems as well as a feeling of integration of body and mind. It helps also to clean emotional wastes from the threads of emotional contact with the world so that the ability to give the self can grow. Some students experience personality changes, and almost all find a sense of unity with others. Some say they become aware of cosmic processes such as the throbbing of particles of energy. Reaching deep within themselves, students find that their basic natures, like puppies, are joyous. One called

it "a constant love affair with the Absolute." Since the enlightenment and wisdom to resolve such paradoxes as "many are one"
must come from one's own mind, not from logical reasoning or
objective study, it is an error to look elsewhere. "Seek wisdom
within," my guru would say.

Recent research has shown that meditating subjects' brain
waves slow from a predominance of the beta waves (fourteen to
sixteen cycles per second) we all use for everyday activity, to
alpha waves of eight or nine cycles per second, interspersed with
even slower theta waves. Yogis who have meditated for many
years and zen masters show a predominance of slow alpha or
theta waves.

There is nothing occult about alpha and theta brain waves;
we all go from the higher-frequency beta level to the slower alpha
level as we relax, several times a day. We also emit theta waves,
four to seven cycles per second, as we get drowsy and begin to fall
asleep, and delta waves, the slowest frequency, when we are in
deep sleep. Electroencephalograms show that the brain-wave
patterns of meditators are more regular than those seen in other
states of consciousness, which is what distinguishes them from
the brain-wave patterns of childhood daydreaming, drowsiness,
or sleep. Subjectively, meditators say they have a sense of well-
being when they are producing a predominance of alpha waves.

A small study at the University of Texas showed that after
meditation, reaction time speeds up, with increased alertness and
efficiency. Other studies showed increased perception and learning ability after meditation allowed the body's overheated com-
puter to rest. Psychological benefits include, in the words of one
student, "a feeling of greater stability, identity, loving and inner
peace." A number of progressive stages are described by yogis
from India and Tibet until they reach visions of the Clear Light.

In autogenic, or self, training with American patients, doctors
reporting in *Biofeedback and Self Control* found that most of the
high-blood-pressure patients they studied needed four to ten
months for the meditation exercises they practiced to be effective; others have reported benefits from only a few hours or days
of training. The results included: slow breathing (an improve-
ment for asthmatic patients), a change in the threshold of pain
until for some it becomes unimportant, increased relaxation;
vasodilation and reduced blood pressure.

After meditation, most patients studied became calmer, ap-
peared more at ease, and felt more relaxed. Interpersonal relations improved as emotional outbursts diminished or ceased.

Insomnia, headaches and lack of appetite were reduced or cured. Training in meditation can help in cases of bronchial asthma; chronic constipation, stomach acidity and other gastrointestinal disorders; disorders of the urogenital system; endocrine problems; skin disorders; and anxiety and phobia.

Both meditation and self-training are based on three principles: reduction of outside stimulation; mental repetition of physiologically adapted verbal formulas (such as the Tantric mantras); and mental activity conceived as "passive concentration." The approach is self-directed, which means that you have an active role and are not dependent on a hypnotist, therapist or guru.

To reduce outside stimulation, the meditation exercises should be done in a quiet room with moderate temperature and dim light; restricting clothes should be loosened or removed. Relax your body and close your eyes, at least in the early stages. Use any one of three postures: lying down, leaning back in an armchair, or a simple sitting position.

The following verbal formulas, called the standard exercises, will help you to focus on a particular bodily function. By learning to concentrate on heaviness and warmth in your arms, for example, your nerves, muscles, heart and breathing are modified and calmed. Your forehead feels cooler. Among the recommended formulas are: "My arm feels warm, my forehead feels cool, my solar plexus is warm. It breathes me. My heartbeat is calm and regular. I am at peace." Use them slowly one at a time.

Keep the formula flowing steadily through your mind in a filmlike way, staying in contact with the part of the body indicated by the formula. Don't worry if outside thoughts intrude, just let them pass and gently bring your mind back.

Meditation involves passive concentration, which is different from the teeth-gritting, eye-narrowing, active concentration we are more used to. Being goal-directed, active concentration requires a high degree of intensity and involves a great deal of mental energy and effort.

In contrast, passive concentration implies a casual attitude both during the performance and in regard to the result. The mind does not race, analyze or calculate. Avoid any apprehensiveness or goal-directed effort as you enter this state of restful alertness. The method is easy and spontaneous. Meditation means being open to the subconscious as well as developing and expanding unused powers of the mind.

A first step used in all schools of meditation training is to think of your breathing and bring it to a deep, even, slow rhythm. As you focus on your relaxed breathing, extraneous thoughts are driven out and you begin to "one point the mind." This may take several hours, days, or sometimes weeks of practice.

Saying a mantra can be helpful to bring on a relaxed sense of well-being, and with practice triggers this pleasant response more and more easily. *Om*, which is said to contain all sound, is the mantra most used in India, alone or as the beginning of longer mantras.

Next begin passive concentration on any one of a number of visual images. Recapture the sense of well-being and warmth you felt while lying contentedly in the sun at the beach or after good love-making. Some students choose to practice color meditation and start by letting their minds fill with colors—a pure orange light, for example, or the colors of the rainbow. Other adepts prefer to imagine a glowing, many-petaled lotus in the crown of their heads. Still later this can be followed by meditation on abstract concepts such as peace, the Great Liberation, or Great Bliss.

You may want to use mantras in Sanskrit, such as the following:

OM MANI PADME HUM—The jewel is in the lotus.
SAT NAM—Truth is my name, or identity.
OM NAMAH SHIVAY(A)*—Being, consciousness, bliss.
OM SHIVA SHAKTI GANGANATH(A)—Shiva, consort, teacher of the Ganges.
OM BHAGAVAN GURUDEV(A)—God, divine teacher.

According to Tantric theory, these Sanskrit mantras work for two reasons: one is their meaning and what this suggests, and the other is the effect of their sound waves. I do know this: mantras such as SAT NAM, said out loud, almost chanted, when the subject has taken a breath and holds it, cause vibrations to echo in every head and body cavity, helping to relax any unnaturally tense muscles.

Once you become skilled at detaching yourself from your worries, you can make yourself a sunny clearing in the woods even when trapped in a dentist's chair.

To use these exercises specifically to increase your powers of sexual enjoyment, meditate on a gleaming Shiva lingam or other sexual Tantric icon, such as divinities coupled in one of the many

---

* These words have a Sanskrit origin but are generally used in a colloquial form like this, with the final A not pronounced.

Yab-Yum positions. While in the highly suggestible alpha state, use the power of positive thinking to recondition yourself as you would like to be.

Skilled visualization allows you to modify your personality by seeing the faults you wish to eradicate and erasing them, then each day substituting the image of the being you wish to be in a radiant frame—an image that grows clearer each day.

Life becomes more meaningful as you learn to see the world as radiantly beautiful and to see others as godlike. Under the storms and waves of daily living the mind is calm, filled with a radiant vision, at first of the lotus, and finally of the Clear Light of the electrical-atomic impulses lying beyond form.

The same principles can be used to awaken and increase sexual powers. If you are a man, I suggest that you visualize yourself as Shiva with a beautiful erect lingam which women will want to worship; imagine the potency that lies in your flaming Muladhara center, which only you can awaken to bring you unimagined vitality for years to come. Why not make your own mantras, to repeat and meditate on: perhaps, "I am getting more and more potent, bigger and bigger, harder and harder."

If you are a woman you have been taught all your life to be ashamed of and inhibit your sexual urges and you probably think your genitals are ugly. Remember the Tantrics worship them, and see yourself as Shakti, the active principle of creation, giver of life and pleasure, with a never-extinguished furnace of interior energy waiting to be tapped.

Male or female, see yourself as a Diamond Being, impervious to harm and ready for Liberation.

Sex problems are connected to attitude, Wilhelm Reich found. Women and men who were afraid to open up and who could not surrender to release the entire quantity of their tension and sexual excitement were left with an unpleasant reserve of frustration he called sexual stasis. Not only can these physical and mental yoga exercises help to break down neuroses and character armor which inhibit spontaneity and pleasure, but they can also train you in the letting go, opening up and surrendering so necessary for accepting pleasure and attaining full sexual release.

Remember, both internal and external practices are necessary in pursuing the Path of Pleasure. The external are far easier to document than the internal, yet a number of spiritual astronauts have left us testimony and advice.

The experienced yogis of Tibet describe at least four progressive stages in their practice, until they reach visions of the Clear Light in the final stage. They tell of developing unusual powers, such as the transfer of consciousness and the ability to read minds; the power to predict death and danger; mental telepathy; *Tum-mo*, or the power to increase body heat so that they become impervious to the Himalayan snows; healing; and *Lung-gom*, increased speed and dexterity.

Besides physical well-being, meditation can lead to *Bhakti*, the mystical experience bringing you to the essential core.

RITUAL MEDITATION   A Tantric guru from Kalimpong, India, gives some suggestions for meditations during the Great Pleasure Ritual, or Vajra Love Ritual (*vajra* means lightning, diamond and penis). This Vajrayana Buddhist rite goes back to the eighth century in Eastern India, where it was especially popular in Bihar and lush Bengal. Bengali monks established Vajrayana Buddhism in Tibet in the eleventh century.

During the ritual, which can be actual or visualized, and is basically the same as the one you already know, a male and female are needed to help each other. Mixing the male *bindu* (*thig-le* in Tibet), or semen, with the female secretions is considered extremely important. The male student beginning the four stages of Vajra-love should be helped by a Dakini, or Shakti, who has been trained in the arts of Realization.

During the first stage the ego of the man identifies with the attractive object, the beautiful and charming Dakini, and vice versa. The guru suggests that the man say, "I would like to die on your body."

Nothing of the whole world remains in his mind. Nothing can distract him from his concentration and loving action. No other kind of meditation could so naturally cause him to forget everything and be rid of delusion as this kind of concentration of Vajra-love. Vajra-love is pure and unreflecting. Through love and loving actions the Nothingness of personality is realized.

In the next stage, male and female reproductive organs touch, the Shakti and Shakta energies pass, and Wisdom Drops are exchanged. During this copulation there is no subject nor object.

The couple may want to try several kinds of sexual asana, or posture, to bring the man into optimum contact with the Great Pleasure Wisdom Nerve in the yoni of the Dakini. Once in contact with this nerve, the man forgets subjectivity and indulges in the feeling of Oneness of love. The personalities of the celebrants are integrated.

When the climax comes, white drops of Compassion from the man and red drops of Wisdom from the woman are united.

If the Vajra-love meditation is successful, the Great Delight of Enlightenment will be experienced after the final emission of the Compassion Drop and the mixing of Wisdom Energy.*

A Tantric Buddhist from Tibet describes another Vajrayana path of Buddhist Enlightenment, with four levels. He suggests you meditate with a picture or statue of a deity and his Dakini in Yab-Yum. The deity invariably holds a scepter and bell, which symbolize the integration of all polarities, such as male and female, Wisdom and Means. The Shakti is the force or potency of the god. The god is thought of as transcendent and aloof, while the goddess is active in the world. He, or his "femininity reflex," holds a chopping knife and skull bowl, indicating that all ego attachment is to be severed and that the skull bowl of renunciation is filled with the blood of Great Bliss.

To get rid of the obscuring poisons—delusion, attachment, jealousy, enmity and egoism—you must constantly discipline yourself to stay in the Now. Experience Nowness. Surrender your self-conscious search to the Selflessness of the Bodhisattva ideal. Wash out the tendency to isolation. Meditate on the acts of compassion of the Bodhisattva. Compassion radiates intense warmth. Feel it.

Second, go on to the stage of being wisdom, rather than knowing wisdom as an external discovery. This stage brings the discovery of the many-colored Mandala Spectrum, each color jewel-like in intensity; here energies are clearly seen in a panoramic awareness where luminosity is no longer external but a part of you. Develop the transcendental knowledge of Egolessness. Remove the wall between this and that, I and thou. The death of Nothingness brings you to the birth into luminosity.

This is the Vajra-like samadhi—the internal experience of luminosity. Colors speak, shapes and movements speak, there is no room for even a speck of dirt. The perception of cosmic energy is intense and overwhelming, almost blinding in its purity. Do not shrink from the Clear Light. Communicate with the universe. Now you will be aware of the destructive as well as the positive aspects of energy.

---

* This meditation is best done when the woman is having her menstrual period.

The next stage is the Mahamudra, or Great Spectacle, in which you see the universe at its absolute level. Here you feel the wisdom of equanimity; perceive the wisdom of automatic fulfillment; experience openness which leads to the union of Great Joy. You see beyond space and time and develop Vajra pride that you are the heroic One. You experience pulsating, diffusing energy and Radiant Awareness.

Explorers of inner space who do not shrink from leaving rationality for the vision of Clear Light will want to learn how to awaken an energy reserve that is untapped in many people—the quiescent serpent power the Tantrics call Kundalini. She allows disciples to attain their fullest potential, and perhaps undreamed powers, by releasing the lotus sunburst in the skull. Kundalini can be awakened during meditation without the help of sexual maithuna and the ensuing electrical explosion in the brain during orgasm, but this is more difficult and rare in recorded experience.

No one yet fully understands the electrochemical activity in the brain that we call consciousness or the changes that sometimes produce ecstasy. Yet the Tantric metaphor of Kundalini's serpentine rise to unite with Shiva in the brain, as an explanation of the subjective feeling of mystical explosion, the aurora borealis in the head during orgasm, has been given scientific support recently.

Dr. Robert G. Heath of Tulane University found that explosive electrical activity actually does take place during orgasm and he has recorded it with an electroencephalograph. Heath called the changes in the septal region in the center of the brain "explosive manifestations at deep sites."* If interested you can look up his article and see for yourself the peaks and valleys and the spindling which are the neurological imprints of orgasm. There is spike and large slow-wave activity with superimposed fast activity. Spiking occurs during psychotic behavior also, but the spiking of orgasm is a distinct, more uniform and continuous wave than in psychotic behavior.

Once familiar with breath control and meditation, the student should begin by visualizing the process of arousing Kundalini's serpentine energy at the root chakra, the Muladhara, which, you remember, lies in the rounded muscular spot between the anus and the genitals. He should bring his breath under control, then during a deep inhalation contract his anus and draw it upward.

* Dr. Robert G. Heath, "Pleasure and Brain Activity in Man," *Journal of Nervous and Mental Disease*, Jan., 1972, Vol. 154, pp. 3–18.

He should then retain this deep breath and bend his head forward and press his chin firmly against his neck and throat. This attitude of the body is called *Jalandharabandha*. After this the student exhales and draws the navel upward until the abdomen is completely flattened. These sucking impulses produce internal vibrations known as "unstruck" sound.

All the while the student visualizes Kundalini responding to the stimulus of the vibrations, awakening and beginning to rise. Uncoiling herself, she releases energy as she passes through each center of stored-up energy (or chakra), until this motion generates great light as Kundalini rises and finally unites with Shiva in the brain, producing radiant visions.

In his book *Kundalini*, Gopi Krishna describes the great beauty of this experience and the cold, dormant feel of his body when he regained rational awareness. He describes a tremendous increase in energy and appetite later on, as well as receiving poems in languages he had never studied. Westerners who met him in Kashmir were struck by the glow in his eyes, which seemed to emanate a spiritual radiance. The voracious appetite for food remained with him always.

A number of authors believe that the Tantrics were not alone in symbolizing the flight of Kundalini energy through the spinal cord, and suggest that this was symbolized also by the religions of Mesopotamia and the Mediterranean world in the caduceus of Mercury—two snakes entwining a rod—and in the snake gods of America.

From the testimony of yogis it seems that Kundalini can be awakened on many levels. Some describe only increased awareness and vitality and do not hear the rushing sound or see the blinding light that so transformed Gopi Krishna's life.

5 Techniques to Keep the Wheels of Ecstasy Turning

SEX IN ITS ELEMENTAL FORM is a biological urge and function; in its highest, it is a mystical experience. As poetry, music, or painting can be vulgar or elegant, trivial or epic, amusing or serious, romantic or profane, sex can be savored in many ways. Sex can be done for fun, as a form of play, as a way to celebrate the wonder of creation, and as a way of feeling at one with the cosmos. It can be an animal discharge, a bottle of wine, so many orgasms an hour, or an oceanic experience.

The tone of some of the most recent books on sex is down-to-earth and humorous, which allows for lightness and detachment in the learning stages. But the higher levels of sexual experience can only be approached with awe.

Recent references to sex as a funny-looking, ridiculous performance are part of the insecure, adolescent attitude many Americans have toward sex. Critic Van Wyck Brooks points out that American literature is largely an adolescent tradition at its best, and at worst it is often sadistic, especially in regard to sex. In contrast, no other literature is as openly pro-erotic as the Tantric tradition. Many of the books on sex had beautiful paintings to illustrate the sexual asanas, or positions. Temples for worship were covered with erotic statues to delight and inspire the faithful. Some of the gods were shown in the heroic act of giving sexual pleasure to many women at once.

Rich erotic tradition in India was not limited to the Tantrics. All adult Indians know something about the Kama Shastra, the teachings about love. The West is familiar with two works on the subject of love, the *Kama Sutra* and the *Ananga Ranga*, thanks to the translations and publication by the orientalist Sir Richard Burton, but at one time there were over one hundred sources on the theme of physical love. Both these sex manuals and poems like those of Chandi Das and Jayadeva were delicately illustrated with miniature paintings. Even religious works contain a great deal of allusion to erotic material. The Tantrics built on the base of this knowledge, refining techniques and positions to encourage ecstatic peaks in each individual's experience.

In most.Western societies there has been one form of legally and socially allowable sex conduct. This sexual fascism permitted only heterosexual coitus in several "natural" positions between formally married persons. Deviators were persecuted. We are, alas, the inheritors of a tradition that put a boy to death at sixteen in New England for bestiality. Sadistic sex laws still exist in most states. If they were enforced, most sophisticates would be in jail.

On the other hand, a great many people have come to recognize the variety of needs and preferences and the right of individuals to find their own path. Anything goes if we do not harm others or ourselves.

Albert Ellis, one of the leaders in the fight for sexual freedom, believes that many people are too sick or at too low a level of development to experience sex with affection and love. Leave them their cold pleasures. But sex with love is the Tantric path to pleasure.

Often primitive cultures are better at managing the unitive life than we. They have kept their sense of the mysterious and sacred about the biological basics of life. The very young have not lost this sense: the son of one of my friends asked, on learning the secret of conception, "When does this ceremony take place?"

Variety is a human necessity in all aspects of life, and particularly in the bedroom of an established marriage or relationship. Fourier, the French social philosopher, recognized a "butterfly passion" in humans and provided for it in his plans. Those of us who have a taste for monogamy had better cultivate variety and keep an element of surprise in our sex life. Make love in unexpected places. Decorate erotically. Go dancing under strobe lights to the pulsating beat of music that never lets up, to disorient you from ordinary reality. Some people turn on doing things we were taught not to do, such as masturbating together.

If a man is too timid and unaggressive, a woman can hint rape and he may delight her by complying.

One of the elements of beauty in a love affair is the consecration of time. Time to do, time to read, time to ponder, to dream, to remember. This is often forgotten in marriage. Perhaps the day will come when housewives exchange erotica and recipes for love feasts as often as they do cookbooks. An extra spice or two may add more in the bedroom than in the kitchen. Most people have a library of cookbooks—why not of sex books?

A woman should not feel shy about taking a leading, but subtle and undemanding, role in sex. Radha made the bed of leaves and risked everything (she was a married woman) for the love trysts she shared with Krishna in the forest. Because women often have more leisure time, they may have more time to think of ways to keep a sense of adventure in a couple's sex life. And yet except for courtesans, who for practical reasons have been reluctant to share their secrets, the burden of expertise as well as the demand for performance in the arts of love have historically been put on the man. In various societies men have used different sexual techniques with their wives than with courtesans. Procreation was the object in the first case, enjoyment in the latter. The paternal and proprietary rights of the male were thought to be better protected by keeping his wife ignorant of sexual possibilities. Now, however, the historical situation has changed. Equality has entered the social picture. For generations poetic writers have compared the body of a woman in the hands of a good lover to a violin in the hands of a virtuoso. The old solo violin theory is out. Now its a duet we're talking about. A male body too can be played to perfection. At last we have come to the stage when a mature attitude of mutual responsibility and give-and-take is becoming accepted.

Learn to revive the polymorphous, overall sexuality you were born with. Do you love to eat? To dance? To move? Then you have great potential. Life-loving people are usually sex-loving people, and sex links you to life.

Following are some techniques we should all be aware of for stimulating the free flow of erotic energy.

SUGGESTIVE SEDUCTION   The Tantric idea of "accidental embraces" is a subtle one. It really means an "accidental" brushing against a person of the opposite sex.

Suggestive talk can be an effective and subtle form of foreplay designed to get at your partner through the head before working on the body. Try it in the morning, if there is time, when you both wake up fresh and strong. Talk about something you read or heard about or saw—particularly if you've not tried it yet together. Many men get turned on at the idea of having two women at once, a theme a woman can elaborate for rewarding results without ever having to recruit a partner. Erotic books are good: try Philip Rawson's *Erotic Art of the East*; page 29 of *The Godfather*; *My Secret Garden—Women's Sexual Fantasies*, compiled by Nancy Friday; and the old favorites. Make gently provocative phone calls to an absent friend and he or she may not stay so absent.

See an erotic film together from time to time, especially if your own powers are at a low ebb, but be careful in your choice. Several men and women friends say they are put off by tastelessly done films, even popular ones such as *Last Tango in Paris*. Better check out an unknown commodity before you go with a new friend you're hoping to seduce.

Reassuring talk can also be an important part of foreplay, especially with a new partner. Encourage your partner to talk about private thoughts, hang-ups, traumatic experiences and worries he or she might have, and try to alleviate them.

KISSING   A basic and vital step in erotic technique is kissing. Originally the kiss pointed to the idea of a commingling of souls, for the breath equaled the life of the person. The Japanese, Chinese and Eskimos still concentrate on the breath rather than a deep probing of mouths, and engage in nasal contact with delicate inhalation of the skin scents and breath.

You may learn to enjoy all techniques, both nasal kissing and deep tongue-in-mouth kissing, as well as tender kisses on the hands, eyes and so on. You can kiss from crown to sole, making up your own variations, paying extra attention to the armpit and genitals, for scent, the navel, the slippery inner thighs and the back of the neck, a particularly vulnerable spot. Most of this is done by all the world, but your own nuances and variations make all the difference. Sometimes draw your partner to you by the hair to kiss inside the mouth, exploring every nook and cranny. In a playful mood have a war of tongues or kiss reverently "as if sucking the water of life."*

* *Ananga Ranga.*

Try adding the throbbing kiss to your repertoire, moving only the lower lip to fondle the lips that are pressing into yours. Or slyly touch his or her lips with your tongue, or take both lips between your own, or have a tongue battle to see who can fill the partner's mouth with his tongue without being pushed out and being filled in turn.

Hours of gentle kissing while you make love can leave your lips slightly bruised and fuller than usual—a fond memory of the experience days later.

Deep kissing, or mouth congress with hardened tongue, is a rehearsal for genital congress and is a way for the woman to enter the man. This allows a double unity during intercourse. Over-breathing and prolonged inhalation of the other's breath and carbon dioxide during love-making can leave you lightheaded and add to the feeling of being carried away as you alter your own chemistry without the risks of a drug trip.

An oral technique that provokes a great psychological sense of oneness, communion and sharing is to pass brandy or some other favorite drink from one mouth to the other. Sip the liquid, then release it into your partner's mouth through a deep kiss. The liquor can first be held in the curled tongue for several seconds, which enhances the feeling of surprise, penetration and release.

LOVE-PLAY Indian erotic tradition has long recognized love-play as a good outlet for aggression. Elaborate games of dominance and submission are played, and although women are considered more erotic than men, some authors advise them to pretend they are being forced or seduced. Women are warned never to demand intimacy, but sometimes to struggle to add to the sexual excitement, no matter how much they want to be taken, appealing to the complex rape instincts of both parties. But when you play be both a lion and a lamb: this sexual aggression is not extreme, and rape is never advocated. Men are taught to win over their women by the most time-tested methods of all, consideration and kindness.

To signal enjoyment and stage of excitement, there are inarticulate noises and ways of drawing in the breath that subtly guide the partner in choice of technique and communicate how close you are to orgasm.

All of us have a sensitive area, full of erotic power and often overlooked, called the Muladhara chakra—a firm rounded area between the genitals and the anal opening. This center houses a sleeping serpent with the power to shoot a sunflare to your skull. In the preliminaries, caress it, tease it, lick it, press, nibble and tap it to arouse Kundalini. Explain Kundalini's importance and call your partner's attention to her flexing so that later during the ritual, samadhi will be the inevitable result. If your Muladhara is not erogenous at first, sensitivity can be awakened.

Don't be afraid to say what you like with words, or show what pleases you with looks or touch. Look at the breast or thigh you want him to touch or guide his hand or mouth to touch where it feels best and use pressure to show if you want it more or less firm. If, for example, you are a man and a woman is sucking your penis, pull her head more firmly toward you if you want her to take it deeper into her mouth.

Gently beating on his chest or back when you're coming can be a good release for you and transmit much of your excitement to him.

Different ways of stimulating the skin are given a great deal of attention in the Tantras and all Indian erotica. Gentle blows are especially good on the Muladhara center; on the buttocks, to turn them pink; on the nipples, to awaken them. Taps on the genitals can be exciting, too.

Controlled love bites, soft scratches and blows—more or less fierce depending on the desires of the partner—are other good ways of releasing aggression and building sexual excitement. This does not mean to draw blood and leave bruises. You may never be forgiven. Lovers' bruises are made by slow, painless sucking, not biting.

Use of Nails   A feather touch with the nails can charge the very roots of the body hair and skin surface all over the body. Keep it up until you feel your partner shudder.

Marking with the nails is an art in itself, designed to arouse and express heights of passion and to leave a token of remembrance. Care of the nails becomes extremely important—they must be smooth and clean. When seen many hours later, the marks help to perpetuate love and reinforce it through memory. Both man and woman should feel a glow as they relive the acts that made these marks, and feel a sense of pride at having stirred so much passion in another human being. (No intelligent man about town would leave conspicuous marks on a woman married to someone else, of course.) In ancient India such marks only aroused respect for the erotic power of the young men and women who bore them.

The Sanskrit and Hindi names for the various patterns of nail marks are quite beautiful. The *Ananga Ranga* describes one of the most charming and effective patterns as the *Mayurpada* ("the peacock's foot"). "The Mayurpada is made by placing the thumb upon the nipple and the four fingers upon the breast adjacent, at the same time pressing the nails till the mark resembles the trail of the peacock, which he leaves when walking upon mud." (Even now travelers see peacocks running wild in Rajasthan and other areas of India.) Men's nipples are sensitive, too, so don't overlook them.

Other marks to titillate and add skillful aesthetic patterns to your partner's body are called by Vatsyayana A Line, A Circle, A Tiger's Claw, The Leaf of a Blue Lotus, and The Jump of a Hare (when five marks with the nails are made close to one another near the nipple).

Biting   Biting was mentioned by the Hindu experts on erotica as another effective aphrodisiac—and here I would translate as nibbling or pressing with the teeth as I don't believe that severe pain is erotic, except to the very few. To avoid hurting your partner in the heat of passion, try the "Coral and the Jewel" technique, when the biting is done with the upper teeth and lower lip, or nibble secretly just inside your lover's lips. You might make a game of decorating your partner's body with a "Bindu Dashana," or dot made by pressing with the two front teeth; "A Line of Points" (narrow bites); "A Line of Jewels" (open your mouth wider); or the "Broken Cloud" (a wide circular bite on the breast); or make a necklace of marks with your upper teeth. Judge each other's work before it fades.

More fierce versions of these scratches and bites are part of the cutting loose and complete letting go of full orgasm. But use care and moderation; no one wants to emerge from bed looking and feeling as if they just crawled through a briar patch. Dogs bite gently in play and so can you; or bite with your lips rather than your teeth as a horse sometimes does, and dig into the lover's body with only the pads of your fingers, not the nails. Never have an orgasm with a penis, nipple or finger between your teeth, as your jaws may clamp and cause damage. Bite his or her long clean hair instead, or the corner of a pillow if it helps you let go.

Marking with the teeth and nails is valuable for the attention it gives to every part of the body (except, of course, the eyes), the stimulation of deep and surface tissue, and the reminder of past ecstasy when pink nipples and lips are slightly swollen and sore days later.

Another reminder the Kama Shastra overlooked is the way a woman keeps a man's warm, fragrant seed inside until suddenly, minutes or hours later, it gushes out like a secret source full of memories.

Feet Feet are an almost undiscovered erotic resource in our culture. Is it because the Greeks devalued them and taught that feet were made of a baser substance than the head? Is it because our ancestors came from cold climates where feet (and the rest of the body, for that matter) were rarely uncovered—and smelled bad when they were?

In the Middle East and India feet are usually uncovered, in sandals, and kissing and washing another's feet is a sign of great caring and respect. Once you finally discover feet, the Biblical tale of feet being washed and dried with long silky hair takes on a new dimension.

Feet are actually one of the most sensitive and erogenous areas of the entire body and play a major role in Indian erotica. During foreplay caress the instep and length of the toes, licking, nibbling and sucking, holding the foot tight because the partner may begin climbing the walls and could blacken your eye with an involuntary kick.

The pads of the big toes with short smooth nails can be used as erotic instruments, as many paintings and carvings of heroic lovers, who satisfy many women at once, will testify. A man can come between the soles of a woman's two feet held together.

The smell of the feet, if not too strong, can be almost as sexy as the smell of the genitals. Indians have long enhanced the smell and feel and sight of feet with musky perfumes, oils, massage and jewelry. Rather than paint only the toenails, they often stain the entire sole and the tips of the toes with red henna. Feet can, of course, be very beautiful, or at least charming.

Hair The Kama Shastra rightly makes a big point of manipulating your lover's hair. You can hold each other by the hair during intercourse, pull it up, or put it between the breasts. Hair can be smelled or chewed or stuffed in a mouth if the room's partitions are thin. Mix your hair together, especially if one is fair and the other dark. Then fondle and arrange his or her hair,

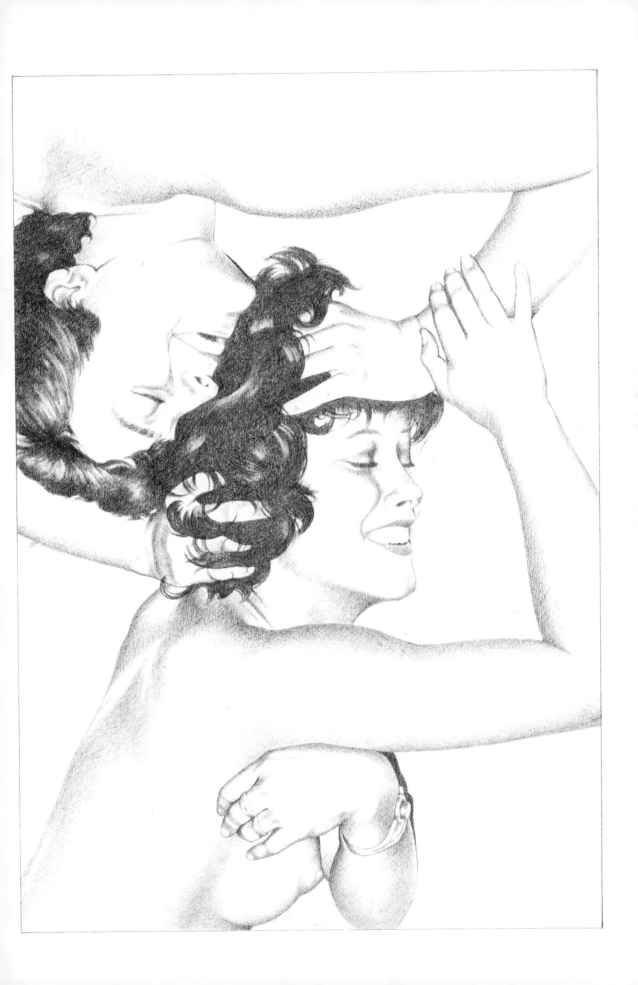

gently running your fingers and nails along the scalp as if combing, gently pulling and lifting the hair to get the whole feel of its texture and sleekness.

Embracing   Embracing is an essential ingredient to any love feast. It can be tender or tough as you become a tiger or lamb at different times. A woman can easily feel rejected if she is not embraced before, during and after coitus.

Don't overlook the seductive possibilities of an accidental touching or rubbing embrace of the bodies—especially if the woman's breasts rub the man's arm or chest—or the socially condoned vertical congress of social dancing, where you can press together. Even standing and talking closer than is usual in our culture can be a subtle embrace of great power. A moving embrace to try is simply pressing your love's forehead with your own, and looking into his or her eyes. You can, of course, embrace with your breasts and thighs.

Embrace like a "mixture of milk and water," as it says in the *Kama Sutra,* bodies entwined until you two can no longer be distinguished.

Massage   Massage and sex go together like the lingam and yoni. Throughout Indian history a whole class of men and women has made a living by practicing this art, usually called shampooing. Whenever possible, massage was part of the daily routine, along with bathing, cleaning the teeth and exercise. Lovers did it to each other and used it for seduction. When Alexander the Great invaded the Indus valley of India he was surprised to find that "the King, while receiving foreign visitors, listens and is rubbed at the same time."

In contrast, most of us are starving for touch. Cats in America, who know they need it, probably get more caressing than most people. Flabby breasts will grow and fill out; loose skin will disappear with proper attention; percussion and firm kneading will reduce cellulite. Trauma and burdens lose their grip, for pleasure is therapy.

If you haven't had the advantage of expert massage, as I did in India, or if you can't remember how it was done well enough to do it to your lover, there are several books on the subject, including *The Art of Sensual Massage.**

You can massage yourself, to a certain extent, as well as your

* Inckles, Gordon, and Murray Todris. *The Art of Sensual Massage.* Straight Arrow Books, 1972.

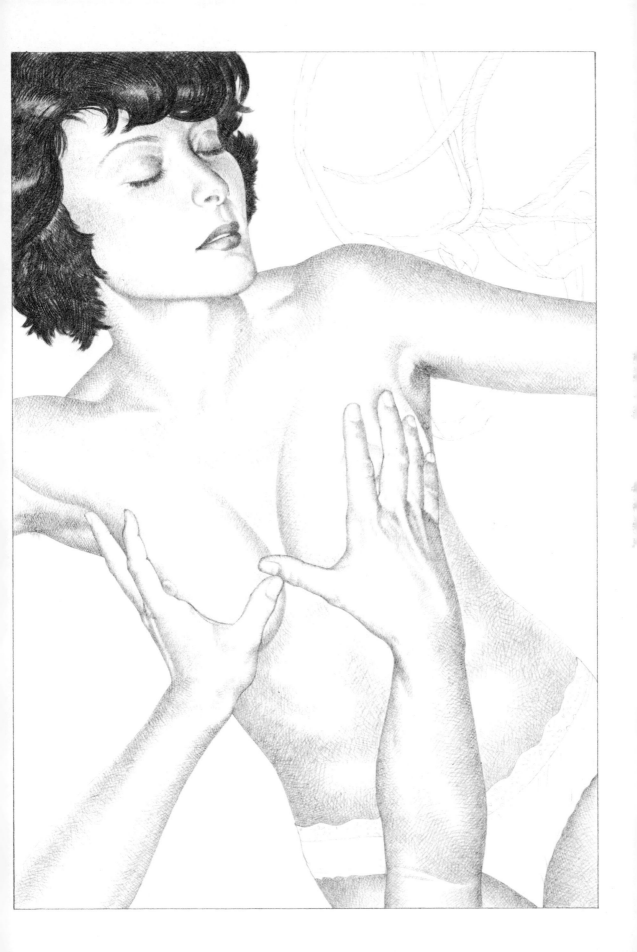

lover, to reduce tension, abort a headache, reduce bulges, and improve skin and muscle tone.

The center of your forehead is a good place to begin: stroke half circles to the hairline with your fingertips while your thumbs press and circle gently on the temples. Follow by pressing with the palm and heel of your hand for ten seconds. Better still, press your forehead into your lover's body when you can. Friction will warm your hands and feet and bring a rosy glow to your face (pat it, head down, to heighten color).

For breasts, lift them and squeeze gently toward the nipples, drawing them out with your thumb and fingers, very much the way the cowherd milks his animals.

Vatsyayana, the author of the well-known *Kama Sutra*, mentions the advantages of massage for lovers as a part of seduction and foreplay. Suggest a massage when he or she feels too tense or tired to make love. As you work, bringing relaxation and an expansive glow to a tired back and neck, you may be surprised at how your lover revives. Work deeply on the lower back and abdomen to loosen a tight pelvis.

A particularly seductive massage includes rhythmically using the flat of your hands, fingers together, to touch the backs of the legs, stroking and kneading, paying attention to the sensitive backs of the knees, down to the ankles and feet, where you stroke the instep and sole, then gently move the bones and pull on each toe. Finally work up to the buttocks, then ask your lover to turn over. Now massage the front and inner thighs where you can see if he, or she, is ready for love. If so, work up to "the joint of the thighs." To increase the seductive element in this special massage, breathe and blow on the skin, nibble on the back, arms and legs.

PENILAMBENCY   Although he listed sixty-four arts of love in the *Kama Sutra*, Vatsyayana neglected the most important one for a woman to know, the art of stimulating and delighting a penis. Let's call it *penilambency*. Women should know how to caress the testicles as well as the penis and be familiar with the most sensitive areas of the phallus. You should love and respect the lingam for the ecstasy it can bring both of you, and handle it gently. Roughness may alienate a man.

Unless the woman has been asked to lead the ritual, it's usually better if she follows the man. Be particularly attuned to his clues after making love once. The penis will often be hypersensitive, and he may prefer that it not be touched for some time, if at all, after a climax. An older man will be less likely to want to make love more than once, and attempts at arousal may leave him feeling that you are not satisfied. If you continue fondling and caressing, make sure that it is done in an undemanding fashion and show no disappointment if there is no response.

The most sensitive areas of the penis are the velvety glans, or head, and the corona, or ridge where the glans joins the shaft, and the delicate vertical membrane that runs on the underside of the shaft from the corona to the testicles. When awakening the penis, the head can be handled, stroked in a circular motion, and the entire shaft encircled and pulled gently but firmly. As it begins to grow, use a rhythmic pulling and stroking, slow at first, then more quickly and firmly. (Because of friction this caressing can be unpleasant or painful, so wet your fingers with your tongue.)

Some men enjoy having their nipples caressed and their buttocks stroked. Stroking the testes is also mutually pleasurable and can be a guide to the degree of the man's arousal. In the excitement phase the scrotum becomes tight, congested and thickened, causing the testes to rise. When orgasm is imminent they will usually be fully elevated.

ORAL SEX: AUPARISHTAKA
Besides being fun, the techniques of oral sex are particularly useful for couples over forty. Unfortunately this group is the most ignorant of oral delights and the most reluctant to learn. Oral sex, like truffles, Italian opera and Campari, is definitely a cultivated taste that becomes increasingly pleasurable with time and experience.

Perhaps the main reason for our often negative initial reactions to oral sex, ranging from hesitancy to outright disgust, is the association with urinating, which may make us think "unclean." The penis is used for this function, of course, but once erect, a muscle shuts a valve closing the opening to the urethra, making urination highly unlikely. Given good hygiene and health, the genitals are more sanitary than the hands, and certainly the mouth. A musky smell is a design of nature to excite and will have just this maddening effect if not blocked by inhibitions.

If we were taught to think of a penis in Tantric terms rather than in the fearful and murderous images of the street—*prick*, *dick, screw, rooting*—there would be no repugnance. The Tantras describe the penis in its unawakened state like this: "The Shiva Linga, beautiful like molten gold, with his Head downwards, tender as a folding leaf. . . . As the cool rays of lightning and of the full moon charm, so does his beauty." Later, in the power of erection, the penis is described: "This Linga is like shining gold and on his head is an orifice minute as a gem. Now he is compared to a sun."

The yoni is as lovingly evoked as the penis, especially in art. Archeologists have found altars for worship in the form of a cunt, named for the goddess Cunti. Elongated holy water vessels in this shape abound in Tantric areas. The yoni is often represented also in the symbolic yantras, or geometrical diagrams of mystical significance.

Oral sex can be enjoyed in many positions. They all burst into my astounded consciousness at once, it seemed, in the erotic carvings on the Temple of the Sun at Konarak, India, during a life-changing visit.

First I studied the large statues of gods and goddesses in the most athletic coital positions conceivable, then lurched into a stone wheel that was equally covered with equally erotic carvings, although this time the scale was small and the positions were comfortable. Again and again unembarrassed couplings were assisted by attendants, who were taking an active part in the enjoyment. Besides the couplings there were definitely triplings, and if memory serves, quadruplings. The statues were so arresting that I was totally oblivious to anyone who might have been staring at me staring at the sculptures hour after hour.

These friezes, called heaven bands, on the erotic temples show athletic versions of the position called 69, the meaning of which is clear if you'll look carefully at the numerals, bringing them together in your mind. The heroic stone couples are standing and acrobatically enjoying mutual oral sex.

Genital kisses like these could still get you arrested in several states. Some of the Kama Shastras speak against what they call *Auparishtaka,* or "mouth congress," and it was taboo in East India and certain other areas. Even tolerant Vatsyayana considered it a low practice, done by eunuchs, masseuses, male servants, women in harems (to each other) and wanton unmarried women. In his opinion it was not fit to be done by a learned Brahman, a minister, or a man of good reputation. And yet he implies great delights when he mentions that for the sake of it women sometimes run away with their servants.

The Tantrics, ever cutting through stultifying taboos, had no teachings against it. On the contrary, certain sects enjoyed heterosexual and homosexual Auparishtaka in unstructured group orgies, while others watched to share in the excitement.

Mouth congress is one of the most delightful ways of practicing the principle, so important to Indian tradition and to good sex, of arousing the woman almost to orgasm before insertion.

One version shown on the temples is worth trying at least once for a different feel during her orgasm. He stands, holding her head down, her legs around his neck, yoni to his face, as the stone guides at Konarak show, for the new thrill of an orgasm head down—mind boggling.

For the same thrill the lazy way, she can lie with her hips and legs on the bed, head and shoulders hanging off and down. He can kneel on cushions if necessary to adjust to the best height.

Sex partners need to communicate: some men like hard stimulation with the teeth that others would consider something out of de Sade.

The tongue can flick, lick and swirl lambently over the surface of the phallus or cunt, and you can use your hands and fingers as well as your mouth. The woman can take the lingam deep into her mouth, "as if sucking a mango fruit and swallowing it up," as Vatsyayana says, using her tongue to lick its head while she uses her index finger to caress the Muladhara sex center. She can cup the testicles with the palm of her hand and use a finger to caress around and around the anus. Alternate mouth congress with hand work since using the mouth and tongue as a yoni can be tiring.

This is a good way to raise a Shiva Linga from the drooping leaf stage to the erect golden stake celebrated in the Tantras. If the man has trouble getting a stiff erection, the mouth of an expert woman can save him from recourse to mechanical devices or inactivity. By sucking and pulling his penis with her mouth she can share the thrill of arousing her partner and be completely sensitive to the amount of suction he needs and likes. One ordinary and unobtrusive device can be useful if there is difficulty maintaining the erection. A rubber band placed around the base of the penis after erection stimulates the major nerves and increases the blood supply. (But don't make it too tight or wear it too long, or it might interfere with normal circulation.) Seasoned women also enjoy being on the receiving end, too. The man can suck, nibble, and use his hardened tongue-tip on her clitoris as he holds her labia back.

For men who have a difficult time coming to orgasm—and there are many, even in their twenties and thirties, who seem to be forgotten in the sex books that teach only how to last longer—the couple may want to try the following combination of oral and manual stimulation. Try this either before penetration, or once you have both become weary from vaginal coitus, or as a reviver after his first orgasm for a second or third if he wants to try to go on. The woman can lie with her head on his thigh and use her hand clasped in one of the several possible ways to work on the penile shaft, while the other hand caresses his scrotum and Muladhara. Since prolonged sucking and caressing with the mouth is tiring to the smaller muscles, which may not be used to such hard work, she can use gentle lip and tongue stimulation on the glans and ridge on the underside, taking the penis deep into her throat from time to time. He can show her just how he likes to have it held and guide her to the optimum pressure and rhythm. This sort of double-barreled stimulation usually can make almost any man oblivious to inhibiting personal burdens, the condition of the stock market, the war in Indochina, and noises in the next room.

Since men too sometimes like to be taken, an inverted form of the Kama's Wheel position is good to use. Push him down on the bed and stretch his arms and legs out like the spokes of a wheel. Pin down the leg and arm on one side with your feet and reach over him to hold down the other arm with your left hand and begin to work with the mouth and other hand. Alternate rhythm for suspense and maximum build-up as you awaken every muscle, every nerve, every cell. Of course, the man can return or initiate the attack. If your head hangs down off the bed you are apt to feel more intensely the explosion in the head during orgasm.

When she knows that he is beginning to come from his clues, his noises and elevated, contracting balls, and she feels the canals from the testicles filling, the woman can take the lingam deep into her mouth again for the mutual thrill of quaffing a jet of bindu. What the psychological thrill to the man is, I'm not quite sure, but I do know it is a thrill. Perhaps imperious pride at imposing himself on her in such an intimate way. As the woman swallows his ejaculate he becomes part of her body, altering her smell later on. This way of letting him become part of her is a tremendously intimate form of acceptance and possession, and some women can do it and enjoy doing it only when they love the man. The taste is not noticeable if the semen is held deep in the throat. It's a good idea to have something cold to drink nearby, particularly if she is new to this and her throat is unsure whether to move up or down.

If she prefers not to swallow the semen, or her throat balks, or if the ejaculation is particularly copious, the couple may find it exciting to let it dribble out of her mouth to be touched with her fingertips for its thick, silky consistency as she gets to know and love it better.

Semen is quite good for you, since his seed is almost all pure protein. Some West African women drink it for the hormone prostaglandin, which acts as a contraceptive.

One of the women in a harem I visited told me that in her area of Rajasthan women were taught to increase pleasure for the man by holding back the foreskin. They gently pinch up a fold of skin at the root of the penis, which makes the skin on the glans even more sensitive and receptive to pleasure. She used this loving pinch during intercourse, masturbation and mouth congress, causing faster orgasm and prompting appreciative noises and comments. In India only Moslems and men who have had some medical problem are circumsized, but the technique can work equally well on men who have been circumsized.

This principle of stretching the genital skin tight works to intensify pleasure in the clitoris as well as the penis. It's good to hold the labia open and pull the mons veneris forward before using manual, oral or penile stimulation. If either one of you takes the trouble to do this before penetration, when the man's body will keep her open, I wager the woman will find that she feels more pleasure. To begin with, just the idea of the man opening up and looking at her most private parts is a turn-on for most women.

SEX SOUNDS   The Indians take great delight in the noises of sex, when they can. A whole cacophony of sounds is used and classified, from the involuntary drawing in of breath when a sensitive spot is stimulated, to hissing, growling, purring, clucking and elaborate birdcalls. Hissing on a wetted neck or behind the ears where you have just licked produces a sensation in itself. Everyone has his own style, from "Oh my God" to yelling bloody murder. One of the most touching parts in *The Leopard* by Lampedusa, compares the reactions of the prince's three women: the French mistress, who was a bit disappointing with *"mon Chat"*; the wild Sicilian mistress, with *"Principe"*; and the wife, who called *"Jesu-Maria."*

Remember to take time for sex as the Tantrics do. Enjoy the undressing, the arousal, the build-up of tension, the prolongation of expectancy, the aesthetic elements of the positions and finally the intensity of orgasm. Nothing is hurried, furtive or ashamed.

MASTURBATION

One of the last common sexual practices to become openly accepted is masturbation. It's still almost unspeakable—few admit socially to masturbation, yet almost everyone does it. Many children learn from the Old Testament that Onan was struck dead for spilling his seed on the ground. Part of the problem is religious attitudes that make sexuality only a distasteful part of the reproductive process. To dualists, sensual pleasure itself is temptation and sin, especially solitary pleasure, which is outrageous. The second negative element comes from teachings that masturbation is actually physically harmful.

Half the medical students from five Philadelphia medical schools polled in 1959 believed this absurdity. I still hear people use the term "self-abuse" and found it in my child's dictionary. A friendly priest who teaches and counsels many young people told me in all seriousness that a friend of his had become mentally ill and had to enter an institution after masturbating one afternoon. I hope my comments on guilt feelings were able to penetrate.

Attitudes are changing, however. A Presbyterian study group published a report in 1970 that was accepted for study by the General Assembly. The report contained this historic sentence, "There is even some argument for the possible *value* of masturbation in relieving sexual tension and attendant physical discomfort in the pelvic region, in contributing to psychosexual development and in providing a satisfactory form of sexual gratification to single persons or to married persons during periods of separation where intercourse would be inappropriate or impossible."

Today many authorities in the field of sexuality, such as Masters and Johnson, do not consider individuals to be sexually healthy until they are able to masturbate. Masturbation is an excellent sexual exercise for keeping pleasure circuits open and responsive, and for releasing tension. Sophisticated women masturbate because it speeds up orgasm so that they can better

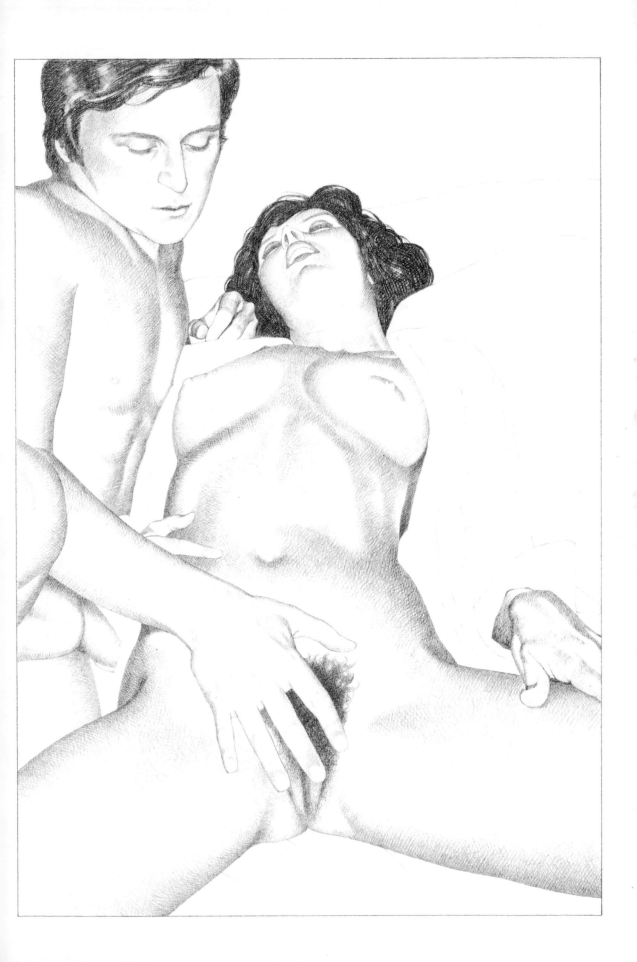

coordinate with the man or men in their lives and because, like coitus, it keeps up their hormone levels, slowing down some effects of the aging process that come from hormone starvation. Sophisticated people masturbate because it feels good.

I don't advise a man to masturbate before a date because it deprives his partner of some of his interest and energy, but this may be a good idea for a girl who is usually slow to respond. She will only enjoy him more. After all, it seems to me the only disadvantage of masturbating alone is that we don't meet many interesting people that way.

How to masturbate is quite a personal matter.

The best way to learn to masturbate yourself is by practice, to find out what feels best and brings you to orgasm fastest. Test to see how many you enjoy having—perhaps it's more than you expected. Or if you prefer to prolong the high before the first orgasm to having several, discover what sort of stimulation gets this result without making you numb or sore. Some women prefer stimulation directly on the most sensitive part of the clitoris; others like to caress the side of the shaft and the whole of the mons and labia for a more gentle and drawn-out reaction.

The best way to learn to masturbate someone else is to experiment to see what gets the best results and most appreciative sounds and movements. Better still, simply ask him or her to tell you, or show you.

If your partner is infinitely sensitive, you can get away with the *Kama Sutra*'s advice to just look at the area you want stimulated; or begin to rub your lover's thigh, start to caress yourself, or ask. If you can't quite bring yourself to say, "a little farther up and harder, please," or masturbate yourself in front of someone else just yet, try gently moving his or her hand and pressing harder where it feels best. In women the sensitive area changes from time to time. If he is masterfully making you numb fast, lift his hand a little for a more gentle pressure.

It's good to sneak up on direct masturbation of the clitoris. First stroke the thighs with considerately warm hands, working around to where the inner thighs join. Still ignoring the yoni for a moment, move back and rub your finger around the anus. With the pad of a finger, firmly stimulate the rounded Muladhara area between the anus and yoni with back-and-forth and circular motions. Gently give a few fingertip taps as well, to begin to awaken Kundalini, causing her to stretch and alert the higher chakras.

Some women prefer the whole hand for masturbation, with

the heel on the mons, the long middle finger on the clitoris and reaching into the vagina (mound of the first joint on the clitoris, and tip in the vagina). If orgasm doesn't come after a few minutes, try opening the lips and stretching the clitoris so that it is raised on the pubis.

If you're a man and your partner is slow, take your time and make her watch while you give quick blows to the clitoris with the pad of your finger, or even the side of your hand if your touch is gentle. Then with your clean, smooth, rounded nails make a pattern of nail marks on the labia and the clitoris. This looks much more violent than it is and usually causes great psychic turmoil as well as pleasure, appealing to an element so loved by the Marquis de Sade yet not sadistic or hurtful. Finally, stimulate the clitoris directly by pressing hard with a vibrating, moistened finger or tongue to finish. Or pull the mons veneris up toward the belly and insert two fingers to work like a thrusting penis to see if she likes the vaginal sensation. (Many women don't feel much.) Or, better still, do them all in turn.

Vatsyayana has a good section on how to use the lingam to stimulate the yoni before penetration. Hold it with the hand to guide it and rub back and forth as an elephant rubs with his trunk, or rub in a circular motion, increasing both speed and pressure and teasing the clitoris occasionally by giving it a hard tap with the lingam. The two organs together are beautiful to see with their colors deepened and intensified from the engorgement of excitement and occasionally a pearl drop of lubricant at the opening in the penis.

A battery-powered vibrator is a modern lover's secret weapon, unknown to the ancient Tantrics and the erotic temple builders, and far superior to the ivory phallus often used in harems. A woman may be too shy to get one herself, even if they are advertised for massaging the face and neck, so a considerate lover might make a present of one to his lady. There are two types to choose from, a plastic phallus and a more expensive mechanism that fits on the hand. (A really thoughtful lover will warm the first model between his legs or hands before touching its glacial plastic head to her most sensitive part.) A vibrator can make her respond faster and more, and be a good bed stand-in when she wants an orgasm and he has just come or is not interested in sex just then, or is busy, incapacitated, or away. Don't forget that it can, of course, be used to massage the face and neck as the ads say—and the breasts and belly and inner thighs and labia and clitoris and buttocks and anus and penis and scrotum and Muladhara—to increase overall skin sensitivity. When the mental and physical stimuli are right, there are no zones that aren't erogenous.

Try it deep in the vagina too. A woman can practice constricting her muscles as the man gently tries to tug it out. This game builds a viselike grip.

Women who are starting sexual self-exploration ought to know that once they become easily turned on and fully orgasmic they can masturbate anywhere, anytime, by tightening their own inner muscles. This pulls the hood over the sensitive area of the clitoris, which will expand and harden from the vasocongestion of excitement, rubbing it ever so gently.

This most subtle of all masturbation techniques uses a woman's own constrictor cunni and levator vagina and is invaluable for quickies, to make sure she is ready to come fast so that her response meets his.

The same subtle self-stimulation is good if a man has hair-trigger trouble (and the couple doesn't have time to work together to slow him down), so that there is no need for him to masturbate her, which would probably overexcite him and end any chance for insertion.

An effective way of masturbating a man is to hold the hand like the hood of a cobra, cup the lubricated lingam in the palm and encircle it with the pad of the thumb at the glans on the sensitive ridge on the underside. Now move the hand up and down from the glans to the root while the other hand holds the scrotum and fingers the Muladhara firmly.

Or hold the fingers like an unopened lotus bud and use just the tips of the fingers and thumb to squeeze tightly around the girth. You can get a subtle variation in movement by pulling harder as your hand reaches the glans, thus milking it as a country girl milks a cow.

Or make a ring with your thumb and first two fingers to symbolize the sacred yoni shown around the lingam in many Tantric icons.

Or rub the lingam between your hands as if making chapaties* or biscuits but be careful to keep it wet and lubricated, as you can produce fire this way.

When you make love to yourself use your head as well as your hands. Sometimes think of your favorite erotic film, or invent one. Look at a book of erotic art, such as *Erotic Spirituality* (a book of photographs of the temples of Konarak), *Erotic Art of*

---

* Thin Indian pancake.

the East, or, if you are sophisticated, the illustrated version of the *Report of the Commission on Obscenity and Pornography,* done by a California publisher, which goes as far as color photographs of women and animals. Read an old erotic favorite or try something new, such as *My Secret Garden,* by Nancy Friday, to give you ideas. Explore *The Indian Song of Songs,* by Jayadeva, about the loves of Radha and Krishna. Choose the beautiful *Gita Govinda* in an explicit translation, such as the recent one by George Keyt, or try a version with Kangra miniature paintings for illustration. Or read the *Ratimanjari,* the garland of love, also by Jayadeva, especially if you are a romantic and like to think that all nature yearns for pleasure when you do. Imagine the warm atmosphere of the gentle forest at Brindaban along the banks of the Jumna, where the hillocks look like breasts and even the orange and mango trees are passionate and the willows droop in hunger and desire. Let loose the sex urge that is concealed in you like the lightning in a cloud.

Or think about a heroic Shiva Lingam, such as the one Shiva had after being shot by Kama's* arrow of desire, flaming so hot that it made the ocean boil when he jumped in seeking relief. A lingam so hot that it can only be quenched by your yoni, as Parvati at last assuaged Shiva's desire.

Invent your own psychodrama. If you're a woman, imagine you are the wife of five men—like Draupadi, who was married to the five Pandava brothers at once—who all take you in turn, each in his own favorite way, while the others watch and then all take you together.

Or imagine that a demon like Ravana is chasing and chasing you through the forest. He catches you finally, ties you down, and rapes you. But unlike Sita, who could not forget Rama, her husband, you enjoy Ravana's advances, tame him, and become his harem favorite. Sometimes when he is away you sport with the women of the harem yourself with large ivory phalli.

Another reel in your own private showing of exotic erotica to get you up there when you're constricted and preoccupied might be to imagine every detail of a secret tryst in the forest with Krishna—the smell of the orange blossoms and jasmine, the moonlight, the bed of flowers, every shade of emotion as desire and anxiety war in your breast. Expand on Jayadeva's words: "It was our first meeting. I was shy. But Krishna spoke tender and flattering words by the hundred. I responded with a soft smile

---

* The Indian God of Love.

and sweet prattle. And he loosened my garment." Imagine radiant Krishna coaxing you gently, holding you by the hair, undressing you, exploring your body and finally make an explicit vision of him making love to you, while the other gopis are searching for you. Will they discover you before you come? Let the possibility of being discovered add tension to the idyll.

Or see yourself as Sita with Rama, returned to the throne. Make love in front of the whole court, who applaud their acceptance when you come.

A man may be all these things in reverse—Shiva with a giant lingam; Ravana with his harem, pursuing Sita; or Rama with Sita as his devoted wife; or be one of the Pandava brothers, and imagine the other brothers with the faces of your best friends.

If you are shy and need acceptance and permission for sex, as many people do, imagine a strong seductive woman, like the intelligent and beautiful Ambapali, who seduces you. Ambapali was the respected, educated and wealthy courtesan who gave Gautama, the Buddha, an orange grove.

If you need a stronger, more dominant image, think of black-faced Kali, who sits on you, making love; who is goddess, mother and mistress all in one. Work out your own sexual acceptance.

As you become more liberated and your own experience gets richer you may outgrow your need for fantasies. You may no longer need to be raped so that someone else takes the responsibility, or to get permission and approval from an authority figure, or need an element of anxiety to increase tension. Later fantasies might be just the reliving of the best love-making you ever had, detail by detail.

Masturbation can, of course, be combined with the oral sex techniques that have already been mentioned.

6 The Varied Positions of Ecstasy

THE ASANAS   The asanas are a series of psycho-yogic postures developed to enable everyone to transcend the ordinary human condition and attain cosmic consciousness by harnessing inner power. A number of the asanas are known to most Hindus—indeed, you may find that you have been doing several of the following asanas for many years. The ever-eclectic Tantrics adapted, elaborated and added to ancient human love positions to encourage the flow of sexual energy. Remember their spiritual aspect as you do the positions.

Tantrics teach that spirituality does not descend from above but is discovered within oneself. Absolute renunciation and denial are useless in this spiritual quest, for best results come from the use of full mental, emotional and physical capacity. Successful practice of the asanas should bring awakening and illumination to help you reach your blazing potential in Shiva consciousness.

Most Hindu love manuals, which the Tantrics use and expand, list five main types of sexual position, similar to positions all over the world, and are often delightfully, if not very erotically, illustrated. These asanas, or bandhas (attitudes), vary with the woman lying on her back (the Uttana Bandha), lying on her side (the Tiryak), sitting (Upavishta), standing (Uttita), and finally when the woman is taken from the rear (the Vyanta Bandha). Each of these groups has numerous sub-classifications which can add enormous variety to a couple's sex life, with subtle variations in angle, depth of penetration and friction.

Sometimes there are strange rules, such as "the man should

always lie on his left side and the woman on the right," which my guru agreed could be disregarded as having no basis other than tradition.

One great difference between Indian sex and Moslem or Western sex is the Indian preference for postures in which the man (and sometimes the woman) squats, sitting on his hams with knees wide apart in a hunkering position. If a person is used to squatting and so has good balance and leg muscles that will not cramp quickly, this offers the advantage of exposing the genitals nicely, giving excellent control, and keeping the pair more alert and aware of what is going on than the prone postures, which encourage drowsiness, even sleep. Indian men, women and children spend a great deal of time hunkering—playing games, getting rid of body wastes, sewing or grinding spices and food grains on a stone on the kitchen floor, just resting, and even perching on walls or tree limbs for hours to watch soccer and cricket games and horseraces. Other Orientals, particularly in the Pacific, enjoy this position for both foreplay and coitus. Hunkering doesn't take long to learn and is great for relaxing around a campfire as well as for sex.

Another difference is India's great fondness for both sitting positions and very athletic ones, as we all know now from pictures of the erotic temple sculptures.

Much of the advice in the extensive Hindu literature on sex concerns kissing and the fondling of hair, breasts, bellies, buttocks, the yoni and lingam. Couples often started their love-play by looking at beautifully illustrated love manuals. The best-known of these here are Sir Richard Burton's translations of the *Kama Sutra* and the *Ananga Ranga*. Actually these books devote more space to foreplay than to actual intercourse, and surely this emphasis reflects a lesson well learned. The aim of such extended foreplay was to hasten the woman's sexual readiness as well as her final paroxysm of enjoyment, while delaying the man's orgasm. He was cautioned to listen to her breathing and love cries as clues to her readiness and eagerness for actual penetration and satisfaction. All authors warn of the dire consequences to marital harmony of using a wife sexually without concern for her happiness and sexual gratification.

Vatsyayana mentions a form of congress where the niceties of foreplay and afterglow are *not* to be employed. This is called "congress, like that of eunuchs." The woman is looked down upon as being of a lower caste or a servant and is used only to satisfy the man's desire.

Here the Tantrics disagree vehemently with Vatsyayana. In their sex ritual, all sex partners, even the lowest caste prostitutes, are not only to be treated as equals but divinized and treated as gods.

Notice how the woman is more than a passive instrument to be played in a solo male performance. She has a full share in the erotic activities, if not more, as the interior activity of her yoni can be constant, especially in the most inactive asanas, such as the Mula Bandha, when the man cannot thrust.

As you read this section notice how the Tantric asanas vary tension and relaxation. The Mula Bandha, for example, would be put last on a scale measuring tension and friction in the build-up of response and so is good for only the most orgasmic pair. This asana requires a couple who, after long practice, don't need much movement other than constricting the vagina to make orgasm happen. They just lie there touching only at the genitals to let it come. Such relaxed coitus to orgasm may be new to many people, but this "let it happen" attitude is particularly Tantric. On the other end of the scale some Tantric positions are the most kinetic and powerful I know. Asanas such as the Yoni Asana are full of tension and friction, with electrical sparks almost flashing.

Both can work or the partners can take turns moving, one representing energy, the other matter, one doing the work while the other relaxes, perhaps alternating the rhythm to tease, surprise and then push relentlessly until they are both seized by contractions. By taking turns you can learn to become excited by less and less physical movement.

Other asanas add movements combining athletic joy in the play of muscles with the elegance and grace of dance. The line of legs, feet, arms, trunks and head are all considered and refined aesthetically. Sometimes a small detail like holding each other's hair up over the head in full tufts adds to the composition.

Beauty of line and form is not the only consideration, of course. Changes in position, angle of contact, and friction do produce different shadings of sensation and increase enjoyment.

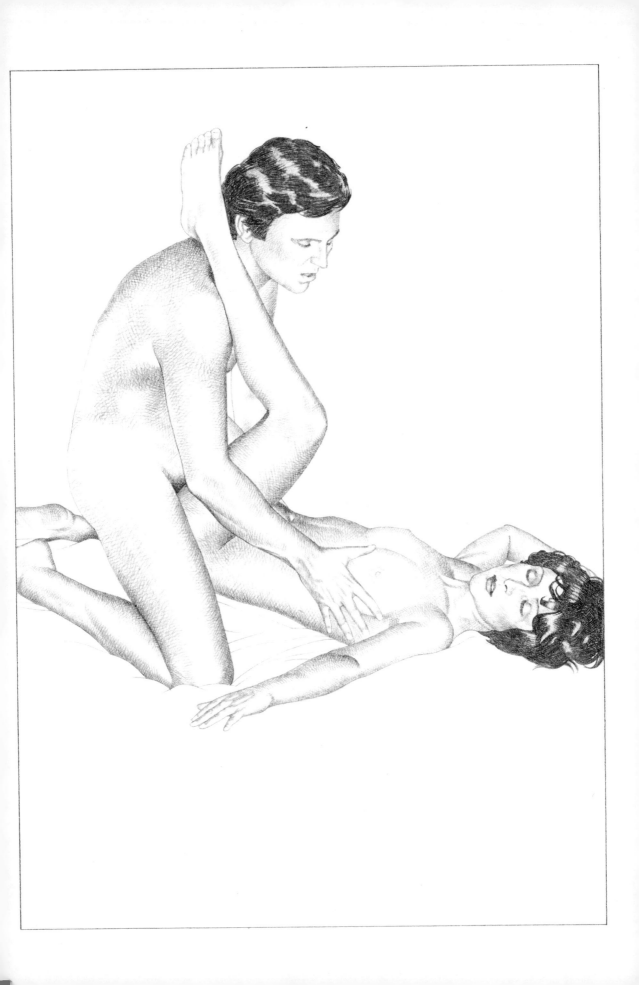

UTTANA: POSITIONS WITH THE WOMAN ON HER BACK

The Indians are not the only ones to like this position. It seems to have been a favorite of Chinese Tantrics, as well as other Chinese, since it was shown over and over in the bridal books given to newlyweds.

The woman lies on her back, lifts her legs as high as she can from the hip joint, at right angles to her body or even beyond, and rests them on the man's shoulders. Her yoni yawns open to enclose his phallus, and her legs encircle his neck and head.

The Samapada Bandha

The Samapada Bandha has two main advantages, especially for women who have been stretched by childbirth. First of all, the penis can penetrate the widely opened and exposed vagina right to the hilt. The second is that increased sensation is produced from the strong double pressure where the downward-sloping vagina meets the erect elastic penis. No matter how distended or weakened the muscles of the vagina have become, strong contact and friction will be produced, maximizing pleasure.

This flexing is excellent for the woman's spine and muscles of her lower back. She may have to exercise before she can enjoy this, but then the rewards are double. A word of caution: this position should be tried gingerly at first to make sure the woman can accommodate the entire phallus, although usually the potential size of the average vagina is more than adequate, unless there are unusual problems.

The man may use one or both of his hands to caress his partner's belly or breasts; the woman can stroke or cup his face if he leans forward, or reach his scrotum.

Less extreme versions of this position can be used when the woman is not supple enough to raise her legs to the man's shoulders, and simply for variety.

For a change, he can lie back between her legs and enter her with his legs opened sideways to enclose her yoni, trunk and head like scissors, to get one of the closest and most stimulating unions possible. Since it maximizes genital contact and is so comfortable, this version of the bandha is excellent for quietly performing the ritual.

Nagara Bandha

In the Nagara Bandha the man grasps the woman's ankles firmly and opens her legs as high as his waist. He can open them wide to make her feel helpless and dominated and get a good view of his strong organ entering her exposed opening, or she can wrap them around his back to feel closeness and draw him farther into her.

Avidarita Asana In the Avidarita Asana the woman raises both her legs and puts her feet on the chest of her mate, who sits between her thighs. The sensitive soles of her feet can enjoy the feel of his skin and body hair, if he has any, while in the beginning her toes can play with his hardened nipples before she concentrates fully on the greater pleasure of his penetration and thrusting.

Traivikrama Bandha Here the woman's legs are opened like scissors, one lying on the bed or carpet and the other raised as high as she can, to his waist, his shoulders, or to the top of his head, while her mate sits, kneels, or squats for entry. This tends to draw the sides of the yoni tight around the base of the lingam, increasing both partners' sensations.

Vyompada Bandha Now you'll see why I recommend starting with basic yoga first to get in shape for the full variety of asanas. In this position the woman lies on the bed or carpet and draws her legs and hips up and back until her knees are on either side of her head and her feet touch her spread out hair on the bed. She becomes nothing but yoni.

Indrani Asana Legend has it that the wife of the Aryan god Indra preferred this. She lies on her back and opens her bent knees as wide as possible (they need not touch the bed), for a feeling of openness and maximum exposure of her yoni, like the goddess genetrix so often sculpted and worshiped in stone. To feel even more exotic, the man should squat over her for penetration.

A variation would have her squat, head upright, with her knees wide open exposing her genitals as an offering to him.

Smarachak Asana, or Kama's Wheel Again the woman is on her back and the man is over her. Both open their legs wide and the man takes the woman's hands so that both parties lie with their arms and legs stretched out to the sides. This gives the man a feeling of domination as the woman surrenders under him, and lovely contact of trunks, bellies and breasts, as well as the genitals. The man's weight causes his pubic bone to massage the woman's fleshy mons veneris.

Saumya Bandha In this old Indian favorite you'll recognize the missionary. The woman lies flat on her back or lounges back on large cushions, while the man either squats over her or lies on top of her. He may embrace her tightly with both his hands behind her back

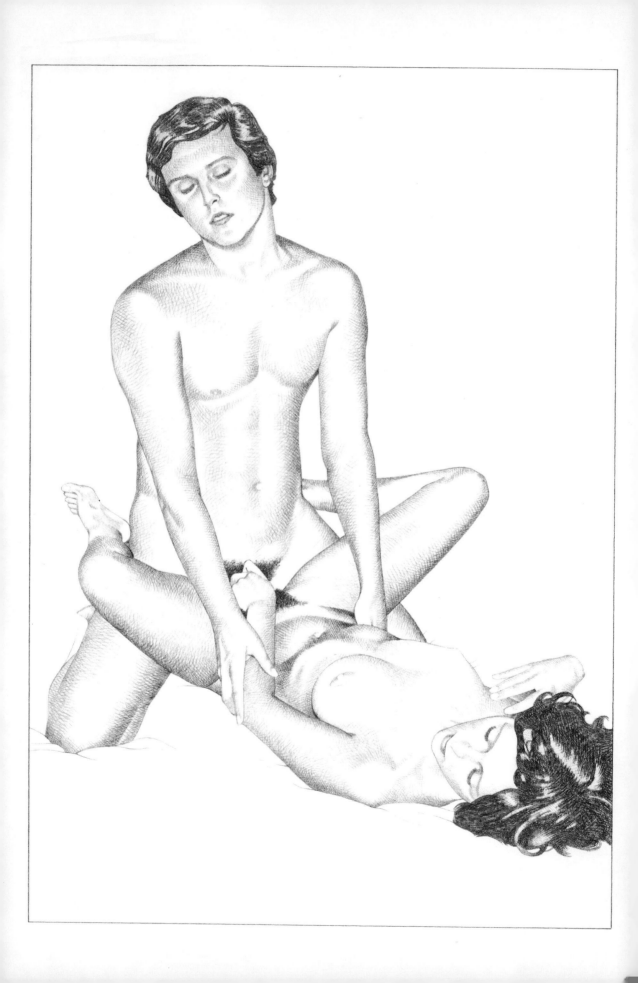

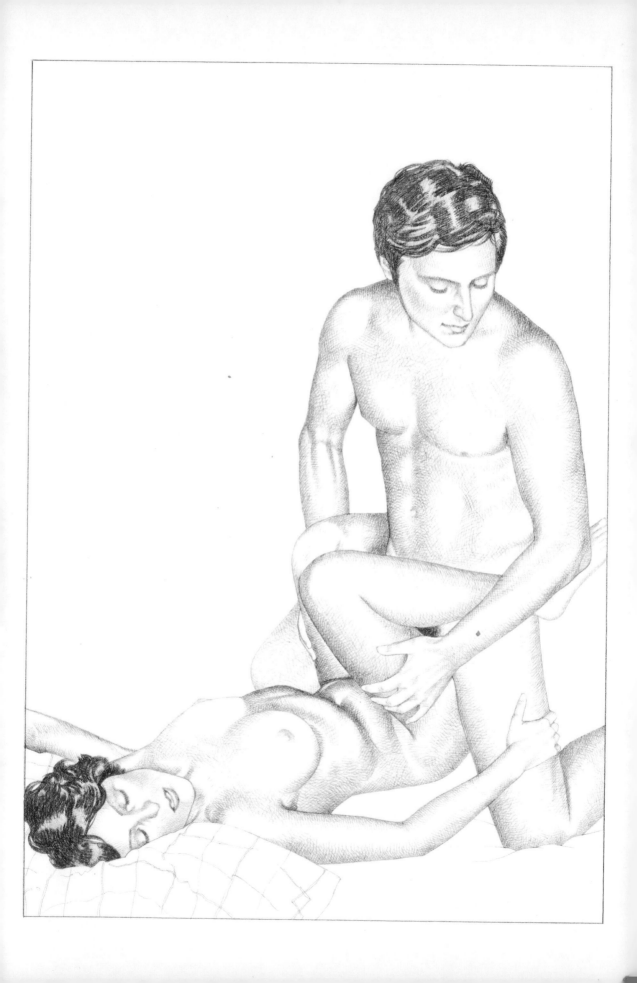

while she hugs his neck and enjoys the sense of closeness. Her thighs can twine around his back or legs so that she moves with him.

Jrimbhita Asana,
or Kama's Bow

The woman lies on her back and the man places a cushion under his love's hips, raising the seat of pleasure and bending her body gently backward into the form of a bow. He may kneel between her legs to reach and penetrate her, or stretch his own body in a vault to cover her as the sky covers the earth.

Sphutma Bandha

Here the man enters the woman, who is lying back, then raises her legs and holds her thighs close together, helping her yoni squeeze his penis tight. The pressing action increases friction.

For variety, these positions and many of the following can be done with the man standing beside the bed and the woman lying with her hips near the edge. She can squeeze and constrict her yoni, milking the man's lingam as he stands and leans forward.

Puhapaka Asana

In this joyous position, the man is on top as both partners lie facing each other, with their legs together and arms over their heads as if they were diving. To allow the man to enter, the woman should first lie on her back with her legs open, knees bent, displaying her yoni fully for his worship, or *puja*, like the stone goddess from Hyderabad. Once he is settled snugly inside her, she can put down her legs and begin kissing his mouth throughout the asana. This position does not allow for the deepest penetration, but offers stimulating contact of the root of the lingam with the clitoris. The woman bears all of the man's weight, so it won't work for every couple.

Mula Bandha

Here there is little contact between the partners and none at all between their trunks. I recommend the Mula Bandha only for extremely orgasmic adepts who have been happily practicing Tantra for months and who are able to attain a high pitch of arousal through meditation and foreplay. To begin the asana, the man sits with his knees open and feet together. The woman faces him and settles on his pleasure organ. Keeping the lingam in the yoni, both man and woman, Shiva and Shakti, lie on their backs with their heads at opposite poles. The woman's buttocks rest on the man's open lap, her legs encircle his waist and they grasp each other's pulsating wrists. In this posture the feel of the increasing pulse rate is the best way they have of sensing each other's building excitement and keeping the passionate energy flowing in a circle before it explodes into their brains. The restraint itself can add excitement, and the unusual angle of the lingam does make for increased pressure on the top of the yoni, which intensifies pleasure, although the lingam cannot go deep. She can constrict and relax in a steady rhythm bringing them both to orgasm.

TIRYAK   The next category of favorite Hindu and Tantric positions is the Tiryak, or side positions, which are very restful to both parties.

Vinaka Bandha   To enjoy this bandha both partners lie on their sides facing each other. He raises his top leg over her hip and leaves the other stretched out on the bed. Because it is so easy for both parties and allows freedom to experiment with their hands, mouths and eyes, this bandha can be prolonged for hours.

Sampata Bandha   Here the two lie stretched out straight on their sides, without entwining. This does not allow for the deepest penetration or maximum rubbing, but is fun for a change when the woman is feeling highly orgasmic.

Karkata Bandha   Here also the couple lie on their sides, the man between the woman's thighs while her legs wrap around his body, making it easier to move in unison. The woman can adjust to be sure her clitoris rubs on his skin and body hair as they clasp each other.

Lata Asana, or Creeper Position   For this method of fixing the mind on a single point the couple entwine each other as closely and as completely as possible. The pair may lie comfortably on their sides or stand. The woman winds herself about her man, mixing her breath with his. If she can lift her leg over his shoulder, penetration and sensation for the woman increases. Fingers caress hair, legs and arms intermingle so as to be almost indistinguishable, like the tendrils of a vine encircling a tree trunk.

The Arab sex book *El Ktab*[*] mentions that the side position was the favorite of Allah, who permitted only four positions for Moslems and frowned on oral sex.

---

[*] Umar Halabi, *El Ktab*, Madrid, Caro Raggio, 1927.

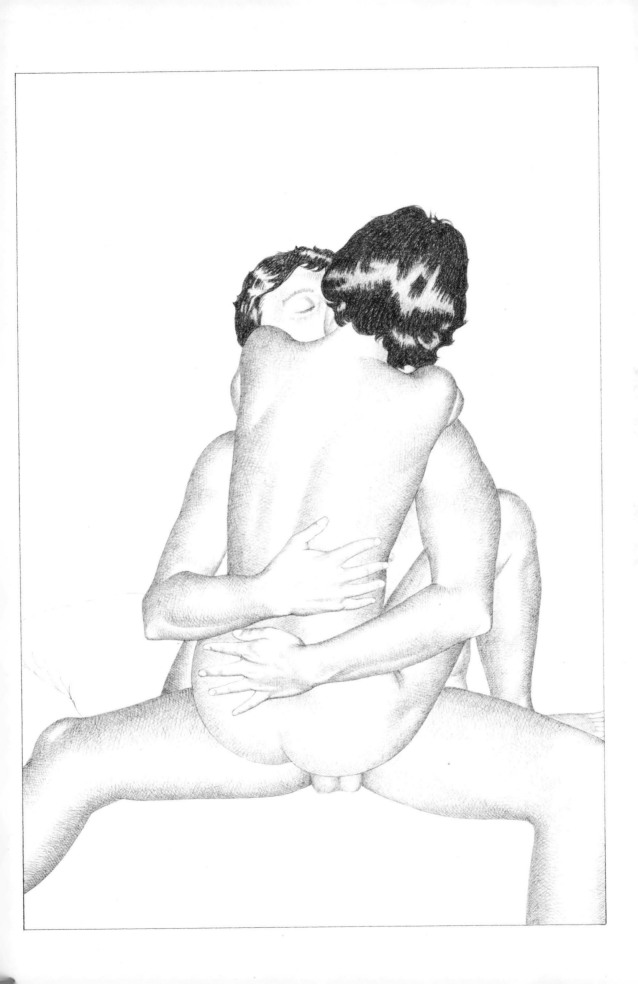

UPAVISHTA, OR SITTING POSTURES
Sitting postures are much more popular in India than in the West, where many people still think that sex is something done under the covers in the dark when half asleep. One reason Tantrics esteem the sitting postures so much is that they are conducive to meditation and visualization without so much chance of drowsiness. They want to remain tranquil but alert to every nuance of sharing and pleasure. No need to sit ramrod straight in these positions. They can be done just as well, and certainly more languidly, while lounging back on cushions.

Padma Asana
The man sits in the lotus position, with his knees open and feet as close to the Muladhara sex center as possible, in the happiness position. The woman settles herself on his stiff lingam, her face touching his, her arms wrapped tightly around his neck. She raises her legs, which pass over his elbows to allow for a piercingly deep penetration. The extended line of elevated legs finishing in drooping, perfumed feet can be as elegant and graceful as any in ballet.

Suhapadma Asana
Thin is almost the same as the Padma position, except that the woman's legs tightly encircle the man's waist as his sex plunges in. The curved bow of her ass rests on his feet.

Rati Asana
The Rati Asana is a favorite of Nepali gods and goddesses. Often the gilded bronze goddess holds a chopping blade high to sever the bonds of ego. The man sits with his legs open. The woman covers all of his sex with her body, except for the balls at the hairy root, still visible under her round, firm buttocks in paintings from Nepal. They look deep into each others eyes, their mouths meet, and their tongues mingle.

This position can be very useful if the couple has to be content with a car seat as the location of their first ritual. In Roman days maidens were often sexually initiated and deflowered by sitting down on statues of the god Priapus, carved in stone, with an erect lingam. Modern versions of this defloration ritual no doubt still go on in parked cars.

Canchala Asana
For this elegant ritual position the man sits facing forward with his feet on the floor. The woman also faces forward with her back to him and sits on his lingam with her legs wound around his open legs and an arm passing back around his neck. The man's hands are free to touch her breasts and clitoris. A mirror will prevent any feeling of remoteness by allowing the lovers to

look into each other's eyes and watch the yoni move up and down on the upright lingam.

Upapad Asana   The woman sits on the man's lap and wraps one leg snugly around his waist, raising the other leg over his arm or shoulder. Care and beauty of the feet become tremendously important in such an asana. The Indians wash and massage them with perfumed oils, color the nails with scarlet lac, and even stain the soles with henna, and usually wear silver toe rings and anklets.

Vaidhurit Asana   The sitting pair wrap their legs around each other to add to the feeling of oneness.

Panipash Asana   Here the couple lean slightly away from each other so that they can hold each other's feet lovingly, caressing the soft soles and insteps, and stroking the toes, especially the great toe.

Sanyaman Asana   This time the woman wraps her legs high around her lover's waist, at elbow level, while he holds her neck in his hands. Each change of the angle of the woman's legs varies the sensation a little.

Koormak Asana—   This time the pair sits with mouth, chest, arms, legs and relaxed
The Turtle   bellies touching and merging, as well as the genitals.

Yugmapad Asana   The man sits with his legs wide apart, the woman faces him, with both her legs passing on the same side so that he can squeeze her thighs together to increase pressure.

Many paintings and line drawings show positions in between the sitting and the supine postures, in which the couple lounges back on one of the large and colorful cushions the Indians love so. In the sitting or lounging positions the man may want to pick the woman up from time to time, if she is light and he is strong, for a few strokes, allowing them both to see the beautiful fusion. He can move her from side to side and back and forth. My guru, who was a tall, strong, athletic man with a tiny, gentle wife, once admitted that these difficult positions made him feel particularly strong and Shivalike. They rarely climaxed this way, but enjoyed it for preliminaries.

Ekadhari Asana   To begin this position, the man sits on a bed, lounging back comfortably, with his legs open and lingam erect. The woman

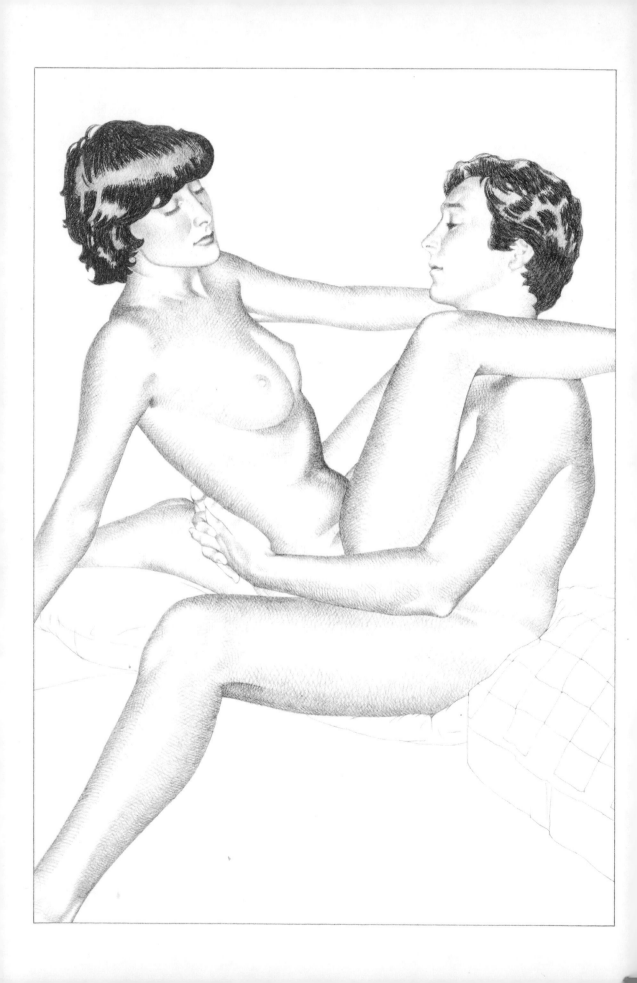

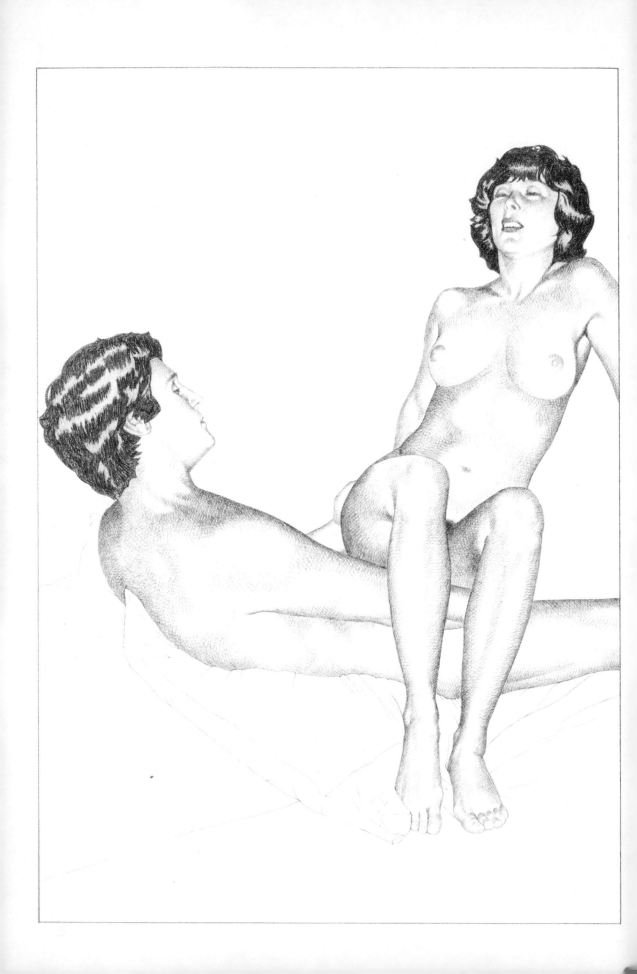

faces in the same direction as the man, with her back to him. She squats over him with her legs open and gently settles herself onto the still stake of his penis. The partners move at will. The man has his hands free to stimulate the woman's nipples and clitoris, which are within easy reach. This position is particularly arousing and unforgettable when done in front of a mirror, where the open yoni is visible as it is filled with the lingam, and you can see both faces during the moments of ecstasy.

Chakra Asana   When you do this, if you can, you will know why it is called the circle position. It requires a supple spine, especially for the man. He enters his Shakti, who is lounging on her side, with her help, then, with his feet toward her head, and facing away from her, he arches his back and bends his head backward to kiss her, so that their trunks approximate a circle. One of his arms reaches back over his shoulder so that he can cup his mate's breast with his hand.

The symbolic circle keeps the energy of the pair from being dissipated and intensifies the shock of pleasure when it steals upon them, for orgasm is an inlet as well as an outlet of energy. Deep penetration is not possible, and in an old painting from Nepal you can still see the pink tip of the lingam as it enters the yoni.

UTTITA BANDHA— STANDING POSTURES   Indian, Nepali and Tibetan art, including sculptures in stone, gilded bronzes and paintings, shows many variations of standing intercourse.

Hari Vikrama Bandha   This form of standing connection is a favorite Yab-Yum position in Tibetan temple hangings, where usually there are coupled deities in the center, often surrounded by supplementary smaller figures. As many of these pictures show, the god is standing with his legs apart and one knee slightly bent, and using one arm to embrace his consort as closely as possible. She stands facing him, one leg standing on the ground or on his foot and the other lifted and wrapped around the thigh of his bent leg, one arm wrapped tightly around his neck and the other raised high. She is impaled on his lingam, with belly and breasts pressing into him and head thrown back in glory. The line and angles of this coupling make it one of the most powerful and electric of all positions.

If the man is much taller than the woman she may stand on a step, a stool or even the edge of a low bed, where the couple may want to fling themselves later in passion.

The shastras, or scriptures, say you'll soon find the Maharaga* this way.

You might want to try this standing position in the shower. You can pretend you are being bathed with infinite gallons of cosmic bindu—warm, unlimited white sexual liquid raining down on you both.

Yoni Asana   The Yoni Asana may also make you feel like a Tibetan god and goddess. To begin this sexual posture the man stands with his legs apart. He can support the woman by holding her feet or cupping her buttocks in his hands as she wraps her legs around his waist. He may bend his knees to help lift her onto his erect organ. Later he may lean against a wall, sit on the edge of a bed or chair, or lay his partner on a bed to finish the ritual.

The Yoni Asana can be patricularly useful if the couple wants to make love in an unexpected place, such as an elevator, where there is no place to sit or lie down. Deities in this position are painted on banners to decorate the walls of Nepali and Tibetan temples, enjoying timeless bliss.

Kirti Asana   This time the man stands and the woman wraps her arms around his neck, nuzzles her head into his neck, and wraps her legs around his waist, hanging from him, while he helps to lift her by holding her buttocks in his hands.

If she is light, try this while dancing (a jiggling, shaking rhythm, like some African dances, is best).

VYANTA ASANA   In this category, the lingam enters the yoni from behind, while the woman stands, bends down, or lies on her face. The man gets to enjoy the focus of rounded buttocks, first by sight, then touch, and can still reach her breasts and genitals.

Bandara Asana—   The animals taught us this position. The woman gets down on
The Monkey   her hands and knees, while the man stands over her. He spreads
Position   open the two moons of her ass and enters her, very gently at

* Maharaga—great emotion.

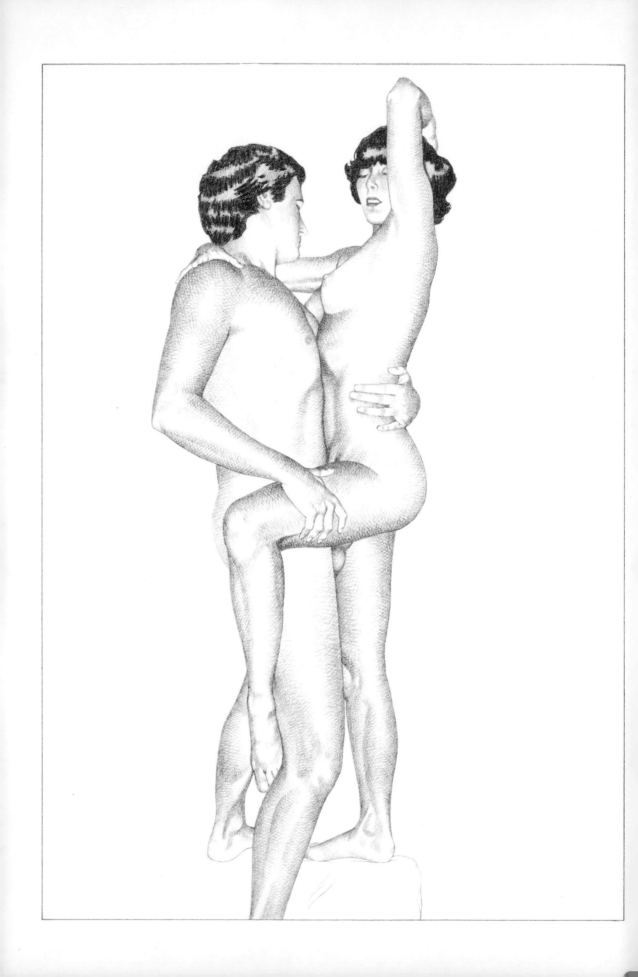

first. The man's hands are free to grasp and pinch her dangling nipples or play with her clitoris. He can remain still to feel her suck and squeeze his lingam with her yoni, or thrust and plow into her deepest crannies as he wills.

Tantrics in Orissa painted a delicate miniature of a couple enjoying this position on a low canopied bed.

Tenuka Asana—
The Cow

The woman stands, then bends forward at the waist until her hands touch the floor or bed, bending her legs a little. She is not on her knees. The man mounts her and comes into her yoni from behind, wraps his arms around her waist, and ruts her like a bull. Remember the cow is sacred in India, so there is nothing degrading in this comparison.

In a playful mood, Vatsyayana suggests this position for one man and several women. Playing at "Congress for a herd of cows" was good for women in harems when they were lucky enough to get hold of a man.

Gajasawa Asana—
The Elephant

The woman lies stretched out face-down on the bed, with her hips raised on a cushion and her legs apart. The man sees himself with the kingly strength of the pachyderm and an organ of enormous girth to match. He lies on her, flexing his back, his hips drawn under so that he can enter her while feeling the softness of the full buttocks she pushes into him. He may first want to play by rubbing his organ between her cheeks and using the tip on her labia and clitoris as if it were an elephant's trunk.

Since these rear-entry positions do not rub the clitoris they are best done to finish off love-making when the woman has already come and is feeling easily orgasmic. The man, of course, or the woman herself, can reach forward to stimulate the clitoris until she is gratified.

Vatsyayana recommends imitating other animals too. "In the same way can be carried on the congress of a dog, the congress of a goat, the congress of a deer, the forcible mounting of an ass, the congress of a cat, the jump of a tiger, the rubbing of a boar, and the mounting of a horse. And in all these cases the characteristics of these different animals should be manifested by acting like them."

In a different spirit, the pair may want to roll to the side for a rest. This is often good for a second or last orgasm, since the man doesn't need full erection.

**PURUSHAYITA
BANDHA**

One of the great Indian experts on erotica, poet Kalyana Malla, author of the *Ananga Ranga,* calls this "the contrary position, the reverse of what men usually practice." Richard Burton tells us that "This position is held in great horror by Muslims, who commonly say, 'Cursed be he who makes himself earth and woman heaven.'" The reverse was true of the Tantrics, especially those in Bengal, who show it more often than any other attitude in their paintings. It was the goddess Kali's favorite way of copulating with Shiva, if we can believe Bengali art.

Viparata Asana

The woman lies on top of the stretched-out man, once she has inserted the lingam into her yoni, pressing his whole body with hers, breast to breast, waist to waist, thigh to thigh. She can squeeze her legs together and move forward and back, at first slowly to tease them both, then faster and faster until they climax. She can also make circles with her hips, churning up more and more pleasure.

*Shakti on Shiva,
or Bhamra Asana
(Like a Bumblebee)*

Bengali paintings again and again show the goddess in this position on her god. The man lies on his back and the woman kneels over him while she helps him to enter her. She can lean forward like Shakti with her breasts brushing her god's chest and look longingly into his eyes.

This position was also a favorite of the Greeks and Romans, including the notorious Messalina, and appeals to the sexually mature for several reasons. It helps the man to last longer and gives the woman more control and freedom to find her own rhythm and pace. The angle makes for maximum pleasure and allows stimulation of the woman's clitoris on the man's pubic bone; pleasure increases if they put a pillow under his hips. The woman can use a back-and-forth or circular motion, or a combination of both. If she flexes her hips back before moving, her clitoris will rub more. This is a very restful position for the man, since she can do most of the work before sinking down into his arms.

As a variation a petite woman may settle herself on the erect penis of a man who lies on his back. She may face him or face away and fold her legs into the lotus position or straighten them out to change the pressures of penetration slightly. The man can move his hips up and down while she rides passively or she can do all the work to please them both.

With the growing awareness that mature sex does not mean

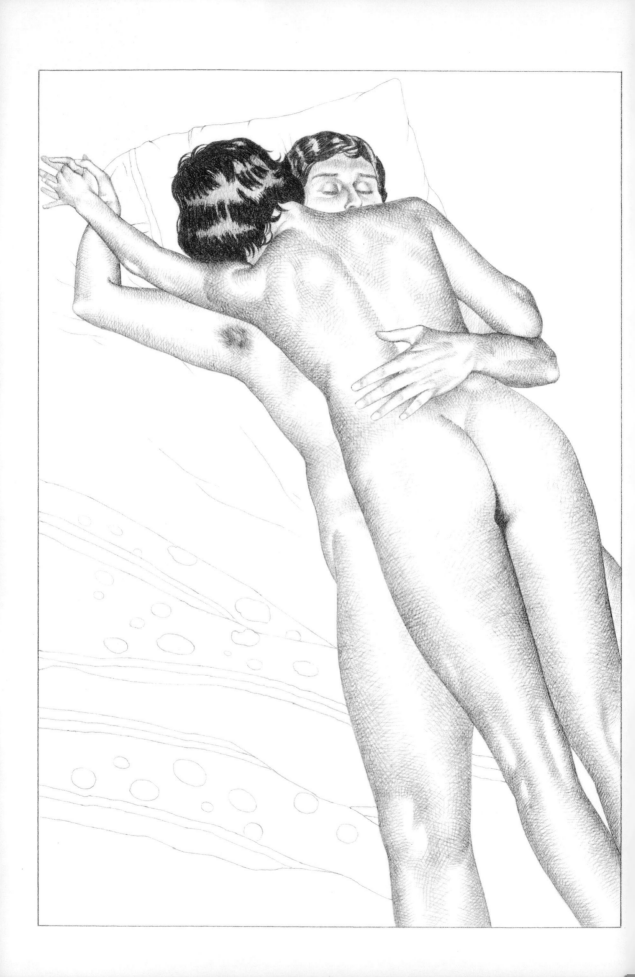

dominance, we may all come to prefer these positions with the woman on top.

In many of these positions either partner may vary the usual back-and-forth movement by turning the hips in a circle like a top, adding an up-and-down movement to the circle, like working a churn, or swinging the hips from side to side. And don't forget the almost invisible viselike movements of the woman's vagina, pressing in quickly or holding for a long time and then pushing down on the penis.

By changing the force, speed and rhythm of all these movements you can produce distinctly different pleasures. The atmosphere can go from the most languidly subtle and sacred to the wildest facsimile of rape.

Don't think that just because I have mentioned only a limited number of sexual positions there is any limit for Tantrics. Half-turned varieties of front- and rear-entry asanas make for a tremendous multiplication, as well as extra pressure from the male thigh on the clitoris.

Keep in mind that Tantra is liberation. Tantra gives you license to think, feel and be erotic, as well as to develop your own ritual variations. Try making up and naming your own asanas.

THE SIMULTANEOUS ORGASM

Although the simultaneous orgasm has been debunked recently as unnecessary, not always preferable, and too difficult to achieve to be worthwhile, I want to revive interest in it as contributing an indescribable feeling of sharing, communion and oneness.

Yes, there are simple ways to bring it on; it is not all accident, as between Mellors and Connie. Pavlov's experiments with the powers of suggestion and conditioned reflex can be extrapolated beyond bells, dogs and saliva to words, humans and orgasms. Once the couple is used to making love together, the man can say "Now" in a commanding voice when he feels himself enter the inevitability stage, which lasts several seconds.

The idea that he is coming will usually cause a spontaneously excited response in the initiated and aroused woman, who can grip her inner muscles more tightly and almost always come to orgasm by the time the man does. The mantra "Now," or whatever the couple prefers, can bring on the remembrance of past pleasures that help trigger present ones.

AFTERPLAY   Afterplay is often neglected by young men. Here an older man can show his skill, civilization and understanding. Afterglow has special importance for the woman, whose orgasmic plateau lasts longer than the man's. A woman can feel shattered if she is left still full of emotion while he leaps up and dresses or immediately turns over and snores. A few words of appreciation, a little attention expressed through caresses, will mean such a great deal to her; a tender look will do. In this age when sex is so often shared without involvement, the words can be noncommittal but sweet and appreciative. Say her name. Now is a good time to stroke her hair, caress her temples, massage her limbs and body, run your nails gently down her back with a feather touch. Avoid touching the nipples or the genitals, for stimulation now may be unpleasant or may reawaken her. For both men and women, this period is one of tranquility and rest. Remember, if there is an unresolved tragedy in your partner's life and your love-making has broken through character armor and released buried pain, the result may be unexpected and perhaps disconcerting if you don't understand what is happening. A primal scream and then sobbing sometimes follow orgasm. This is a good time to hold your partner in a reassuring and comforting way.

Afterglow is a good time to enjoy smells. Many women love the particular odor present at this time, coming from the semen of a beloved man mixed with her own secretions. The odor of his semen coming from her own body can remind her of him hours later.

The *Kama Sutra* mentions a number of little attentions for this period. Vatsyayana recommends that neither partner rush to leave, but that first the man should manipulate the woman's hair, then rub her body with sandalwood or another fragrant oil. (She, of course, can return the favor.) Then, if she has come to his home, he should introduce her to any friends and servants in the house and they should sit quietly talking before they part—there is no shame to rise up once desire has been assuaged, and so no furtive parting.

7 The Subtle Art of Prolonging Ecstasy

An Orthodox Tantrist prevents himself from ejaculating quickly during the thirty to sixty minutes or more that he keeps his lingam in the yoni, by means of certain yogic methods learned during years of practice. He uses both mental and physical control in this process, tensing his spine and pressing his chin into the top of his chest, perhaps even putting his tongue down his throat. There is a much simpler technique for a Westerner, with a less agile tongue, who wants to postpone ejaculation. All that is required is a cooperative Shakti to help a man prolong the pleasures of arousal and achieve a more intense orgasm.

For a woman two factors are important in building up and drawing out pleasure: having a considerate and accomplished partner, and being awakened to awareness of her inner sexual powers. The optimum sensation mounts if she has the advantage of both. Techniques for increasing a woman's threshold of pleasure are explained under the heading of vaginal exercises. The ability to contract these inner vaginal muscles while building up mental stimulation allows some women to experience orgasm more easily than others. Psychic arousal and satisfaction are far easier to achieve when a woman's sex life has been active. With a male organ to grasp, pleasure is even more intense and becomes indescribably more so the longer it is in her, to the point where she may lose consciousness.

Women can show men that they too can enjoy sex longer than they realized, with cooperation. This will hopefully reduce the envy of female multiple orgasm that some men feel.

The couple must talk, and communicate by touch and signs as well. Once the man has an erection his partner can help him to maintain it with just enough stimulation to keep him from losing it and yet help him to keep from ejaculating as long as he wants. The method is the squeeze technique recommended by Masters and Johnson as a cure for premature ejaculation. Let's remove the stigma of inadequacy from this practice, since very good lovers may want to use it to intensify and prolong ecstasy. When the man feels near to coming before he wants to, he should withdraw from the vagina or mouth. The woman should hold the hot penis as if she were picking a favorite flower, perhaps a tuberose, with her thumb and first two fingers. She holds the penis where the head and shaft meet. Her thumb should be on the frenulum, or underside, and her fingers on either side of the ridge where the glans and shaft meet. She should then squeeze firmly but gently for three or four seconds. The man may lose some of his erection, but after a brief pause the penis can be aroused again in a variety of ways, such as talking, caressing, sucking. This can go on as long as the man wants: three, four, or five times. When the man has had enough and is ready for orgasm, he will find that it is of the utmost intensity. Once he realizes he can last longer than he imagined and gets used to prolonging pre-orgasmic pleasures and knows how to recognize when he is approaching his point of no return, he will be able to delay his orgasm mentally. Saying "I want it to last" when he feels the inevitability stage approaching can help postpone ejaculation, damming up erotic tension for an even more powerful orgasm later.

There are a number of cautions. Don't be impatient when you try to attain long-lasting ecstasy. Don't try for records. Sex should always be noncompetitive and undemanding. A man may not be able to come at all if he tries too hard, and the same is true for a woman. The time schedule is only a guide to show the possibilities that exist and that some may be unaware of.

8 Love for the Twentieth Century

Never say you are mine, say only you are with me.

In the West we have been taught to negate the self and think first of others. But one of the earliest Indian Upanishads says that love starts with the self. "In sooth, a husband is dear—not because you love the husband; but a husband is dear because you love the Self. . . . In sooth, the gods are dear, not because you love the gods, but because you love the Self. . . . In sooth, the whole world is dear—not because you love the whole world; but because you love the Self."

The approach in the Upanishads is basically, If you can't love yourself, you can't love anything else. Although love starts with the self, it leads us out of the self. The Tantras taught that you should love the universal in the self, in others, and in the world. Love may lead to wanting to lose ourselves in all life through service and mystical experience.

This idea of the importance of self-love, stated thousands of years ago in the Upanishads, is surprisingly close to the findings of modern authorities on mental health. Abraham Maslow, the psychologist, wrote that people with the most ego strength are the least selfish in their concerns and actions and the most able to love in a healthy way. Only with a strong sense of self, of our own identity, can we feel full enough to want to give love, can we attain intimacy. The more unsatisfied needs and hungers we have, the more difficult it is to be concerned beyond ourselves. Modern love is open rather than exclusive. Today a criterion of mental health is the expanse that the circle of a person's love can encompass. Love is not a pie that is lessened when divided and given away; love is rather a yeasty organism that grows and expands the more it is given. Loving is a habit, a way of being. While all love begins with an emotional stirring within, healthy love is far from the emotional binge so often mistaken for love. To be healthy, it must grow from one to include many and be tempered with knowledge, reason and caring.

Loving is its own reward, creating both the lover and the beloved. Knowing that one is loved helps the self-esteem and self-acceptance of the beloved by providing an ideal image of himself and fostering the belief that he is worthy of love. He is encouraged to grow in the direction of the lover's perception. Love is not always blind; actually the depth of caring allows us to perceive both faults and strong points more clearly rather than less. In fact, aren't we often moved by the very faults themselves —the insecure gesture, the crinkles at the eyes, the freckles, or some idiosyncracy?

The miracle of it all is the way another most imperfect being, who may have pimples or crow's-feet (or both) can make our hearts burst with love for all life, make us feel the common thread that binds us to everyone who has ever loved.

The more secure and autonomous lovers are, the more the element of hurt and hostility in traditional love is lessened. The strong lover, and all of us in our strong moments, can be tolerant and amused at the faults and oversights of the other, rather than personally wounded. Loving is not a cannibalistic feeding on another human being but tuning in to one's soul.

Satisfying our own needs so that we are not overly demanding in our love for our mates, our friends, our children, anyone, is a complex subject and a life-long effort. Doctors and therapists are taught to be careful that their needs for love, entertainment, sex and excitement are filled to avoid the temptation of turning to a patient or patients. Mothers have to be careful not to lean too much on their children. Outside interests and pets help.

Love is the realm of the healthy; of the hero, the Tantras say. If mothers can lead the way and show how to love from strength by being full of interests and happiness, perhaps "I love you" will no longer be one of the most frightening confessions in the English language.

Tantrics are less afraid of emotion than we; they cultivate the Maharaga—the great emotion. Kama, the god of love, shoots arrows marked "open up" and "surrender." Open to love and to life, to feeling both joy and sorrow. Better by far than fearfully killing love and the life impulses is the approach that universalizes love to include all humanity, or sublimates it through art.

By feeling at one with all hearts in the realization of our common emotions and sufferings, we obtain a degree of detachment and protection. Love can also be transformed and enjoyed as aesthetic emotion. Art, either the attempt to produce it or the appreciation of it, can raise love from the realm of passion and sorrow of the worldly plane to the realm of serenity and contemplation. Both the universalization of love and its abstraction in art help to detach us from its pain. Being aglow with our own energy of love is always worthwhile. Life blazes anew with magic and enchantment. Unused powers are awakened and we strive for perfection. The power of love can make life meaningful and worthwhile under even the worst of circumstances, which is the lesson learned in Bengal.

The concept of love as its own reward allows us to go beyond the refusal of the Sensuous Woman to love a selfish man, since loving transforms us. The story of Don Juan has fascinated writers and composers largely because of the effect he had on the women who loved him. Loving and losing, then, doesn't have to be harmful if it makes us grow. Women are right to love themselves loving.

9 Liturgy for a Group Sex Ritual

TANTRIC GROUP RITUALS using sex as an aspect of worship have been practiced in India from Vedic times, centuries before Christ. The rituals varied widely and included the purely symbolic sexual experiences of nuns and monks in Nepal; highly organized cults under the strict control of a guru; and, at their most extreme, wildly orgiastic expressions with no structure at all. Some rigid cults in the second category did not allow young men to ejaculate and taught methods of retention of semen. A young man who just let go could find himself humiliated in front of his fellow disciples, in a spirit at odds with my understanding of Tantra. Such misers of semen certainly disapprove of the orgiastic cults (as in Bengal) where semen was and is copiously spread about.

Exaggerated theories about semen played an important part in both the more common ascetic path, advocated by most religions, and the Tantric Path of Pleasure. To both groups, particularly in ancient China, India and Greece, semen represented divine sexual energy. The ascetics, whom Philip Rawson calls the sexual misers, taught that semen should be retained selfishly to increase one's own power. Buddhist Tantrics of the Vajrayana school of Nepal and Tibet were a hybrid group who recognized the benefits of harnessing sexual power and the exploding pleasure of orgasm, but who also wanted to hold on to their semen. They practiced methods of retaining semen, for a while at least, by retrograde ejaculation into the bladder.

The Hindu Tantrics are sexual spenders like the free souls

mentioned later in this chapter. These "red" Tantrics* believe the more sexual activity the better, for it only increases the world's store of divine sexual power. This theory is part of the reason for temple prostitutes, who are said to take divine status from their husband, the god, and extend it to the populace. The Chandogya Upanishad sets forth the idea that the universe procreates with every copulation.

Among the sexual misers are groups who wanted to set themselves above average people and so seized the idea that hoarding semen adds to the individual's own spiritual powers, making themselves a superior class of celibate priests.

On the other hand, the cults of Ishtar of Babylon, Astarte in Phoenicia, Isis and Osiris as well as Ptah and Pasht in Egypt, Shing Moo in China, Aphrodite and the Gnostic Sophia in Greece, Jupiter and Juno and Vulcan and Venus in Rome, all stressed the regenerative aspect of sex in nature. A lusty Canaanite harvest-time hymn to Baal illustrates the views of one cult of sexual spenders who hoped to increase the yield of their crops:

> Effect unions in the land,
> Diffuse love in the earth,
> Pour out well-being into the midst of the earth,
> Increase love amidst the fields.

Regimented behavior was suspended and man's sexual drives were freely released without harm to society during bacchanalian festivals associated with the fertility cults once prevalent in Egypt, Babylonia, Greece, Rome and India.

Many Temples in India were dedicated to Surya, the sun god. Now only a few temples of the sun remain, but at one time Surya's worship was widespread. A characteristic of the architecture of temples dedicated to the sun god is the erotic sculpture that forms part of their decoration. Orgies involving several people and even animals were recorded in stone on the temples of Khajuraho in North India. The overall impression these temples give is of great beauty and majesty.

The aim of worship is the same in all these variations—to lead to the experience of divinity. All three types of cults—where sexuality varies from symbolic participation to controlled rites to orgies—continue in India, in Europe, and in the United States.

Various sects argue as to whether the single-couple or group

---

* Ascetic Tantrics are called "white" Tantrics, sexual Tantrics are called "red" Tantrics, and the few cults that have practiced black magic are called "black" Tantrics.

sex rituals are more effective when done between married partners or outside a legal bond. Majority opinion favors the latter
as being more exciting and so leading to greater exaltation, but
there is no rule.

The spring Holi festival, celebrated all over India, is a symbolic
reminder of certain ancient group sexual practices. Almost everyone takes part in playing childish pranks, singing bawdy, suggestive songs, and throwing red powder or water on passers-by.
To many, the red color has a sexual significance. So do the songs;
my requests that friends translate them brought only blushing
refusals every time.

I spent two Holi festivals in Calcutta and a third in Rajasthan,
generally in hiding. I had seen other blondes, including my
daughter, who spent months after the celebration with their
porous hair colored various shades from red to pink. During my
third year in India, my husband and I were invited to spend Holi
with the families of a Maharaja and a Rao Raja, who were both
excellent polo players. Once I asked another polo player the
difference between the titles Maharaja and Rao Raja. I got a
one-word reply: "Bastard." The Rao Raja was the son of a harem
favorite, not a legitimate wife, who by his own personality and
skill in polo playing had become a favorite son and inherited
lavishly. Before going on to Jaisalmer we stopped in red Jodhpur
for a few days. We were invited to join the Rao Raja and one of
his sons while they practiced polo on the expansive field in front
of the red sandstone palace every morning. The area was flat,
and the full moon and the red ball of the rising sun were both
visible at the same time as we rode. Then we sat in the marble
pavilion between the field and the palace while turbaned men-
servants gave us tea and breakfast.

The father told me more of the Krishna legend which is connected to the Holi celebration. There are several versions. In his,
this blue god, one of the many incarnations of Vishnu, grew up
among simple cowherds who lived in Brindaban, along the banks
of the Jamuna River. Krishna is a favorite of poets, who em-
broidered tales of his feats as a lover as well as his heroic acts in
killing demons. A gentle musician, he lured the women, or gopis,
of Brindaban into the forest with his flute playing. There they
surrounded him. To tease them, he disappeared and the women,
suffering from the separation, ran looking for him, crying in
despair and anguish. Their yearning touched him at last, so he
returned and again played for them while they formed a dance
around him. The mood of yearning grew more and more frenzied

until finally the magical Krishna multiplied himself and went off into the forest to copulate with and satisfy each woman. Thanks to his powers, no woman knew he was with the others and their husbands thought they were still at home.

I had read poems describing the erotic details at great length, so this allegory of man's relation with God was not new to me. But the Rao Raja added that in his youth there was promiscuous sexual license during Holi, in public as well as in private. He had often seen groups who would form the round dance around a musician and eventually pair off into the park to consummate their desire. This was not promiscuity as we understand it, for it symbolized the spreading of semen, regarded as the divine sexual joy-juice or energy. During Holi even dignified and beautiful Maharanis are sometimes thrown into a swimming pool by a mischievous relative. The Rao Raja admitted to having done exactly that. Later he drove us to the golden city of Jaisalmer for Holi.

Jaisalmer looks the way towns mentioned in the *Arabian Nights* should look but don't.

Once a wealthy trading post, Jaisalmer shares with larger Jodhpur an unusual unity of aspect and construction. Each city clusters at the foot of an acropolis. In both cases this high stone plateau provided the building material used for the fortress and on all exteriors; even the gravel and sand on the streets come from the same stone, of a deep red color in Jodhpur, and gold in Jaisalmer. I remember no wooden construction, no signs or rusty metal breaking this homogeneity. Jaisalmer boasts extensive carving on the homes of merchants, covering facades and balconies that reach across narrow streets almost to touch, as well as on its three palaces.

A delicately carved palace looks down on the city and two lacy palaces from a fortress on a high rise of golden sandstone. Usually semi-deserted, Jaisalmer was alive for the festival. The Maharaja invited us to come to the city palace after sightseeing, for the celebration. We returned to a courtyard surrounded by stone walls carved to look like Belgian lace. Drinks, including Chivas Regal and a native rose-petal drink of incredible potency, were being served to the neighboring Rajput nobles and army officers. Except for me, the women, brightly dressed, with parasols, were all on a balcony looking down on us, very much separated. Two musicians played music which was twanging and vibrating to periodic peaks, around a huge vat of colored water in the center of the inlaid stone floor. Soon the men started throwing water on each other, singling out my friend, who was from a rival Rajput clan. In self-defense, he picked up a large dipper and began throwing water as hard as he could. When done with a virile man's full strength, this can hurt. Soon everyone but me was covered with the symbolic sexual liquid. I tried to keep aloof from the fun, in the interest of protecting my blonde hair. Finally we said goodbye to the red, dripping, panting Maharaja. Suddenly he seemed to focus too clearly on my still unspoiled, virginal appearance and said something in Hindi to one of his servants. Before we had finished the pleasantries, the servant returned with a bowl full of red powder for the Maharaja, who was still shaking my hand. From the gleam in his eye and his mumbled words about how nice blue eyes and pink hair would look, I gathered who the powder was for—and ran.

I ran up the stone stairs and through long narrow corridors to more stairs, with the Maharaja in full pursuit; behind him pounded my friend and courtiers. I was only getting deeper into the palace, dangerously near the bedrooms, I realized. Finally I stopped running, as I had no desire to do actual research into the private orgies of the present-day Rajput rulers of Jaisalmer, and received two handfuls of red powder, rubbed into my face, hair, chest and laughing mouth. Later, in spite of repeated scrubbings when I drove back to Jodhpur, then Jaipur, to fly back to Calcutta, though my teeth and skin were no longer pink, my hair stayed that way for months and months, a reminder of Holi in Jaisalmer.

The unstructured celebrations of Holi in India contrast with the Tantric yoga classes taught by Yogi Bhajan at the Ahimsa Ashram in Washington, D.C. No sexual intercourse is involved in the teachings of this ascetic school of "white" Tantra, but sexual energies are aroused between the students, who are paired off into couples of all ages, and stare into each other's eyes. By taking advantage of the energy differences between individual men and women, they are able to build up more energy in these two-person Tantric exercises than in ordinary yoga.

Few Westerners have been initiated into the strict cults, but the principles of Tantra are free to all. Many practices become acceptable with the adoption of the Tantric ethical criterion of harm—"If there is no harm there is no wrong"—and the positive spirit that encourages the cultivation of peak experiences. For Tantra raised the pursuit of joy to an art form. A few orgiastic Tantric cults exist in California, more openly perhaps than those in India.

One reason for secrecy has been suggested before. The Tantrics were usually a small minority living outside the caste system of traditional Hindu society, which had an anti-pleasure and anti-worldly bent. The Tantrics were often verbally attacked and persecuted. Further, the path of the Kaulas, the lefthand path, has never been considered suitable for everyone; it is only for him who is called *Vira*, or hero. The great build-up of energy and its subsequent release is considered dangerous to those who are not ready, as are the drugs and alcohol which are sometimes used.

Group sexuality has a long history of expression in Indian art. From the early terra-cotta reliefs of Bengal, dating from the second and third centuries B.C. and showing erotic scenes with two or three figures, to contemporary carvings, group sex is widely celebrated.

On the temple of Lakshmana in Khajuraho groups of seven or eight omnisexual Kaulas cavort. One of them is simply watching; however, he is not more than a foot away from the oral pleasure his friend and a woman are sharing.

A miniature from my Rajasthani friend's rich collection shows a nobleman making love to five women at once; three squat to connect with his lingam and toes while two stand with their legs apart and his fingers in their yonis. All are smiling serenely. This scene of real life is outdone by wood carvings from South India in which celestial male figures were shown in sexual contact with as many as seven floating female figures, using their tongues as well as all other protrusions.

Women, by the same token, satisfy more than one male at once, but never as many as seven. One carved figure bends forward to allow a man to enter her from the rear while she reaches to caress the lingam of a man in front of her. The most I have seen is three—a woman holding two huge lingams in her hands and another in her yoni.

Authorities mention that one reason for promiscuous rituals is the desire to avoid the stigma of sterility and the dangers of possessiveness. Another reason is to symbolize the fact that during a maithuna ritual the participants, whoever they may be, are representatives of the gods and therefore equal. During these Tantric ceremonies the members of the group are seated side by side in a circle, without regard for caste or relationship. In one of the Tantras, Shiva speaks of his wife in the following terms: "All men have my form and all women thy form; anyone who recognizes any distinction of caste in the mystic circle (chakra) has a foolish soul." The rigors and inequalities of the caste system made this physical contact particularly daring in India.

An Englishman born and raised in India told me about the rites of a certain sect that border on black magic. A young virgin is first bathed and anointed by the women in the group. Then comes her sexual initiation, when she is entered by each of the men present in front of the others. The men usually do not come at this time but wait to be with partners of their own later on. Sometimes a stone lingam is used for defloration rites similar to those of the Roman Priapus whose virgin followers sat upon his erect phallus. Until recently tribal people in Bastar state used a realistic phallus with lamp at its base to deflower their virgins.

Another form of ritual involves one experienced older woman who initiates several young men into Tantra on the same night. She is called *Bhairavi*, or female guru. She need not be beautiful, but it is assumed she has spiritual power. An Indian woman traveling through Paris initiated one of my friends, a mathematician, and three of his friends, a year ago. This experience with several men may be envied by sophisticated women who know that they can have almost unlimited orgasms, that waves of pleasure can build up, each one more intense than the last, with the shock becoming stronger and more shudderingly vibrant. This sort of experience would make a woman highly orgasmic, with a hair-trigger response, one might say. These would be deep vaginal orgasms, contributing to a form of self-discovery, self-unfolding, that most women are denied.

Men also had their opportunity for multiple contact in ancient Tantric practice. In one rite they *symbolically* fucked as many as a hundred and eight women in succession.

I have seen a number of temples in Orissa decorated with voluptuous female heavenly figures, the Apsaras, with their bodies bent seductively and their vulvas and clitorises in view. Many of them have holes in their yonis made by the symbolic sexual contact of thousands upon thousands of male worshipers, who wet their fingers and touched the vulva before entering the temple to pray. At a temple in Ellora, which was cut out from the surrounding stone like a sculpture rather than built, my guide pointed out where a touch hole had been cemented up in recent years in an act of bureaucratic prudery.

I've only read about a less appealing form of group initiation, in Bengal, where disciples drank the semen of their guru, which represented his spiritual power. Warm semen in the heat of passion is one thing; cold semen from a cup is another!

But why group sex, after all, even if the ancients did do it, when single couple sex is so wonderful? Is there anything to be gained by something that goes so strongly against our own monogamous traditions and religious teachings? Yes, I think so, for some people. Some advantages have already been touched upon. Group sex can replace the selfish turning inward and away from the world, common among couples who "forsake all others," with a new spirit of inclusiveness and enjoyment in a congenial group. It can be a here-and-now experience of great depth, bringing out the basic similarity and equality of people. At a high level, it can break the boundaries between self-ness and other-ness. To the ordinary joys of sex can be added a sense of communion, mutual support and encouragement, plus the stimulation that comes from watching others and the satisfaction of performing for others. Odd numbers can be accommodated— three, five, seven, or more—so no one need be left out of sexual pleasure for lack of a permanent partner. In this case it's good to have a vibrator handy.

In watching and being a part of a group my friends say they appreciate the art of love even more than usual. One spoke of how watching the tensions of embracing bodies can have the power of psychodrama and aid in the release of inhibitions. Also, far more energy and arousal can be built up by a group than by only two people. In an experiment without sex, I have felt this energy sweep around the room, washing over each individual in turn, and I can imagine how the same phenomenon could pass around a circle of couples contributing to a more explosive and ecstatic sexual release, making it easier to attain the Maharaga, the great feeling.

Certainly it is a good escape valve for monogamous monotonies, which legitimize dependency in narrow, shrinking, concentric circles; where sex is barter, linked to gold rings, silver, linens and children; and people are treated as property. These group rituals put sex on a level of symbolism and enjoyment, where the intense feeling is appreciated for its own sake, and for the personal reassurance that it brings.

Allowing people to let off steam periodically often benefits monogamy, and American swingers say, "the couple that swings together stays together." Loosening inhibitions and breaking taboos in this way may allow them more growth as they break down barriers of personal separateness and exclusiveness to attain openness and intimacy with a variety of people. Why should these peaks of physical and emotional generosity be burdened by feelings of jealousy or shame?

A sense of personal enrichment comes in taking possession of our own body and giving it where we choose. In this way we may become more independent, realizing that sexual pleasure is not dependent on any one other person. It comes from ourselves. Eventually, once the experience becomes internalized, the adept will not need any outward crutch to experience the peaks of ecstasy.

Centuries of Hindu and Tantric experience show that a loving, caring sexual relationship is possible with many people. Why should a group encounter of this profound nature diminish the flow of love in a more permanent relationship? Nothing is taken away. Loving builds love. An experience of this kind can stimulate and increase the power to love, actually reawakening, revitalizing and deepening the permanent relationship, enhancing the total climate of love.

A point rarely mentioned is that group sex is a way to express the homosexual tendencies many of us have, and to explore catholic, omnisexual appetites. My friends who have participated in group sex tell me that women are more likely to enjoy each other's bodies than men are. All the reports I have of heterosexual group sex agree that male participants don't show any affection for each other or even touch. I do know a man who described homosexual, all male, group sex, so this form exists too. Yet surely many men are attracted to group sex by the possibility of enjoying the closeness of their own kind, even if men cannot admit this to themselves in our culture. In contrast to ancient Greece, where men were freely homosexual, most men in the United States and Europe have been taught to fear and despise their homosexual urges. Sodomy is too foreign, too unnatural, and must be painful at first for the passive partner. Group sex might help such men to work through their fears of male contact and to integrate any homosexual tendencies. Strictly speaking, however, Tantra does not encourage homosexuality, and a Tantric group would always end with normal heterosexual congress.

Many Americans are experimenting with variations of group sex. Sandstone, a nudist sex commune in Los Angeles's Topanga Canyon, has institutionalized the orgy. Some members practice reverse fidelity by never repeating a sexual experience with the same partner, always moving on to a new one or ones. Although I have not participated in group sex myself, the following are reliable reports told to me personally.

Willowy Cherie, an American dancer with large brown eyes,

told me about the summer she, her show-business husband, David, and friends Larry, Carol and Anne had a different experience from the no-involvement types one usually reads about in books and articles on group sex. All five people, in their early twenties, lived and made love together for four months while they were doing a show in California.

Actually the story Cherie told in great detail begins in New York. Carol, Larry and Anne came to spend a few days with Cherie and David. Larry and Carol were married and had been living with Anne for eight years.

After dinner the second night Larry and Anne were still talking in the living room when Carol came into the bedroom where Cherie and her husband were lounging on the bed. Cherie had started to undress and had taken off her tight bikini underpants and knit top, but still had on her brown suede skirt. Her long white thighs rose seductively out of the high suede boots she was still wearing. While they were talking, Carol came and sat beside Cherie and put her hand on Cherie's small breast, commenting on how beautiful it was. Cherie was struck at how much she enjoyed this tiny hand caressing her and spontaneously kissed Carol on her open, smiling mouth. Carol became more aggressive and pulled up Cherie's short skirt, opening her long slender thighs.

The women's erotic acts excited David, who plunged forward to kiss the exposed area and hold Carol's tiny breast at the same time. Carol lay down on her back to put her hand around the erect lingam rising out of his pyjamas, and put the tip in her mouth while she started taking off her pants with her other hand. Cherie impulsively helped pull off Carol's pants, and for the first time in her life shyly kissed a woman's yoni, barely looking at it, then drew away, amazed at feeling fierce lust for a woman for the first time in her life.

David turned to Carol and began to make passionate love to her. Then Carol took hold of Cherie's small buttocks and pulled her yoni down onto her aggressive tongue, holding her firmly by the buttocks for several minutes until she shivered and came just a few minutes before Carol moaned in release. Soon Carol felt David tense and explode inside her. David lay back to rest and watched while Cherie, a bit more initiated and curious, examined Carol's body. Gingerly she put her head between Carol's legs and used the same tongue flicks Carol had used on her a few minutes before. She enjoyed feeling enveloped by the soft smooth thighs cradling her and squeezing her more firmly as she worked. Carol's turmoil gave her a new sense of power, which drove her to burrow deeper and deeper, bringing Carol to another orgasm in front of David's eyes.

Enveloped by their excitement, David had another partial erection in record time. Carol saw his member jump, then fall back flaccid on his thigh. She nuzzled her face close, put her head on his thigh, and began teasing his glans and frenulum with flicks of her tongue. She had such control of her tongue she could make it seem to fibrillate against the resting penis. Again it seemed to jump and she took it, still soft, deep into her mouth. As it grew hard it filled her mouth and pushed down at the entrance to her throat, half choking her while it added to her excitement. Now that he was aroused again, David pulled Cherie up on top of his body to penetrate her in what he knew was her favorite position. First she sat very quietly, letting her yoni adjust to his member, then started to move forward and back, faster and faster. He was so deep in her he seemed to reach her navel. This time she threw her head back like a Tibetan goddess and let out a low scream of ecstasy before falling limp on his out-stretched body. Laying her gently on her side to sleep, David, still erect, pulled Carol to him and laid her face-down on the bed and entered her from the rear, moving until they both came. All three slept in a snuggled tangle.

In the living room, Larry and Anne had sensed what was going on and made love rather conventionally.

The next night they all began joking about the "happening" and Larry asked Cherie, only half seriously, "Do you want to?"

"Sure," answered Cherie, dead serious, and walked up to him. He pulled her to the floor in front of the others. Soon Cherie reached out her hand for Carol to join them, then David and Anne followed and the five-link chain began. It was sex so sweet and free and full of pleasure they reached new highs of enjoyment.

Since they were good friends and enjoyed each other's bodies so much, they decided to take a house together when they moved to California for a show. During these four carefree months they made love in a variety of ways. Sometimes only two women were home together, sometimes a man and a woman, sometimes three, sometimes four, and most often all five of them explored the erotic possibilities of the situation. Often Cherie felt engulfed in an unspecific ocean of pleasure, no longer knowing where it was coming from or who was stimulating her. At times one of the group would pull away to rest and watch the others. Several times they recorded their passionate moments with a Polaroid camera. Cherie says her first reaction was, "That can't be me!" when she saw herself caught on film at the center of the erotic group.

The situation must have been particularly stimulating for David and Larry, since Cherie says they made love to all three women whenever all five were together, but the men never touched each other.

Making love to another woman, or several other women, can be mind-blowing to a woman, Cherie says. "At first I kept thinking over and over, My God, I'm kissing another woman—and I like it. I'm holding another woman's breast, a woman is making me come. I kept thinking, This is how my breasts feel when they're caressed, this is how my body reacts when it's stimulated and when it climaxes, this is how I taste. She is so like me."

She was attracted by the fragility of the other women, and their desire to please with no concern about making a superior performance just to show off. And yet she prefers men, much prefers men for their strength, their irreplaceable sex organs, and themselves.

The five parted when their careers took them on their separate ways; the two couples stayed married and Anne moved on. Cherie and her husband returned to New York. Actually strain had been developing in the group over control of the kitchen. Anne, who perhaps felt insecure without the ties of marriage, wanted to rule the kitchen, and her possessiveness began to dampen the sexual relationship.

Cherie and other friends who spoke to me about group sex struggled to express the unique feeling of loss of self and unity with others when the barriers between individuals became indistinguishable. None of these friends had heard of Tantra before meeting me, but they described the same experience of oneness that Tantric mystics describe and the ancient Kaulas found during their ritualistic orgies, the same egolessness that is the aim of all yoga. In their open-minded experimentation, my friends had stumbled on an ancient path developed to tear each individual out of a sense of separateness, isolation and withdrawal, into undifferentiated pleasure and exhalted feeling, when individuals seem to merge.

Cherie's words were, "It's hard to describe, but I would sort of forget about myself. I used to read in books about how the heroine 'abandoned herself to passion,' or something of the sort. . . . I abandoned myself to the group."

These friends again proved that the "lure of the flesh" can

have a transcending function. The ultimate physical intimacy with others can sometimes (no one pretends it happens always), with the right attitude, lead to the experience of oneness and cosmic compassion, at least temporarily.

Another Tantric element in this group experience was enjoyment without attachment. These were moments with no element of grasping, when those involved were sometimes free of envy and possession.

Since part of the attraction of the group sex experience was its newness, it was not addictive, and Cherie and David are so well satisfied at home that they have not gone out of their way to repeat the experience. These friends are not the typical seekers after group sex, who prefer it because they cannot relate closely to one person and fear emotion. Nor was this a coven of strange night people. They are curious, healthy, moderately successful business and show-business people who sometimes enjoy giving their beautiful bodies freely and savoring others in the same spirit. They feel no punishing guilt.

The system of packing women together in harems in parts of India with little to do and little heterosexual satisfaction fostered female homosexuality. The great Hindu epic the *Ramayana* makes this seem understandable—and delightful—though the description there bears little resemblance to the sad, wan relics I saw in an actual harem, which was no longer in use by the Maharaja.

This is Ravana's Harem as seen by Hanuman, the monkey king in the *Ramayana*. Ravana is the demon king who steals Rama's wife, Sita.

> Hanuman saw innumerable women lying on rugs, dressed in every kind of clothing, with flowers in their hair, who had fallen asleep under the influence of drink, after spending half the night in play.
>
> Their breath was subtly perfumed, impregnated with the aroma of the sugar-sweetened wines they had drunk, and caused the sleeping Ravana deep delight. Some of the girls savored each other's lips repeatedly as they dreamed, as if they were their master's. Their passions for him aroused drove these lovely sleeping women to lose control of themselves and make love to their companions. Some slept in their rich garments propped on their bracelet-laden arms; some lay across their companions, on their bellies, their breasts, their thighs, their backs; clinging amorously to one another, with arms entwined, the slender waisted women lay in sweetly drunken sleep. The interlaced groups

were like garlands of flowers attended by lovesick bees, like inter-
woven creepers with their clustered blossoms opening to the caress
of the spring breeze, or like the intertwined branches of great forest
trees full of clouds of swarming bees. So seemed Ravana's consorts, and as they slept closely entangled it was impossible to
tell whose were the bangles, scarves and garlands that encircled
their limbs. As Ravana slept the radiant beauty of his women,
like golden lamplight, played upon him. Some were daughters of
royal sages, of giants and celestial beings of whom the warlike
giant king had taken possession as consorts when he had defeated
their relatives. Some had come to him of their own accord from
love, and none had been forcibly ravished who had not fallen in
love with him for his prowess and vigor, and none belonged to
another save the daughter of Janaka [Sita] whose heart was set on
Rama. None lacked nobility, beauty, intelligence and grace, and
each was the object of Ravana's desire.*

This charming male chauvinist fantasy ends on the dubious
note that the women are happy with their lot.

Cherie's small intimate group, which started spontaneously
and engaged in repeated contacts, is quite different from a larger,
more impersonal group scene that was described to me, and
which might have a special appeal for sexual athletes and those
who want no emotional involvement.

The description a writer gave me of a larger group sex encounter (or orgy) might make it more understandable to the
uninitiated who wonder how on earth the people in the *Playboy*
orgy cartoons might have gotten there, and give practical tips for
someone who wants to initiate an orgy among friends. Frank
was visiting California to do an article when he got a call from
a lawyer he knew, who casually mentioned that another lawyer
was inviting people to an orgy. The caller explained that the
writer would not have to participate if he was not so moved, but
that he must come with at least one girl. Since his wife was still
on the East coast, he invited a reporter who said she was also
interested in observing, but not participating at that time. (They
did take part at a later date.) She was a little worried about being
forced to submit to someone or having to hurt feelings by re-
fusing brutally, but the host assured her that the group was
well-screened and sensitive enough to recognize another person's
lack of interest, and would be fully self-policing if necessary.

The party, for forty people, took place in the lawyer's large

* As quoted in Philip Rawson, *Erotic Art Of The East*, Minerva Press, 1968,
pp. 62–3.

home overlooking the lights of Hollywood, among professionals between thirty and fifty years old. It began like any large, elegant cocktail party, with good food and drink. As they ate and drank, people selected partners the way they would in singles' bars—by eye contact and conversation. Nothing more happened for more than an hour, until an outgoing small blonde woman took a male friend by the hand and led him to one of the large bedrooms. As she went in the door she turned, smiled and waved to the group. About ten minutes later, another couple and then another and another followed them into the same large room to the king-sized bed. When my friend went in he saw the first couple resting back on pillows, watching a group on the lower half of the bed. A girl lay with her knees open and feet off the bed, with one kneeling man performing oral sex on her while another man had his mouth on one breast and a woman put her head next to his to suck the other one. A couple stood at the foot of the bed watching, murmuring, "I think she's ready to come."

The lawyer who invited Frank had practiced restraining his own orgasm, as the Tantrics do. He mentioned wanting to be with every woman there, so allowed himself one orgasm at about midnight and another one just before four A.M., when he went home. Another sexual athlete, an actress, had sex, and presumably orgasms, with almost every man there.

One woman, who had never before had sex with more than one man in a limited period, exclaimed, "I never knew such heights existed!"

By about eleven o'clock some of the guests, in various stages of dress and undress, began drifting back to the living room, where one of the guests played the guitar and sang folk songs in front of the lighted fireplace.

Although it has great appeal for people inclined to voyeurism and exhibitionism, for sexual athletes, and others who are bored or have a sex problem at home, such as an impotent husband or disinterested wife, and for those who want no emotional involvement, group sex is certainly not for everyone. Some men have told me they're not sure they could perform in such a public situation (like the hero in the French movie *Le Sex Shop*) and no doubt the same is true for some women.

Many people feel that group sex is sinful, outrageous, or simply not worth the trouble. An unmarried girl who gave it up after several encounters said that she found it distracting to have more than one person stimulating her. Critics say the lack of privacy and involvement are dehumanizing. I'm not trying to make any converts, but only to add to the understanding of practices that not only exist, but seem to be increasing in our culture.

If you wonder if you could enjoy group sex and want to try the Kaula path to the transcendent, try to visualize it first. Imagine a group of your friends or congenial strangers. Then imagine the necessary mood of self-abandonment, which casts out shame and old notions of social decency. In my own fantasy I can better picture group sex with people I know or at least have met and feel comfortable with before sexual demands are put upon me. I mentally enjoy pleasure and beauty of all sorts, including other naked female bodies as well as male.

Friends who want to initiate unstructured group sex might invite the hoped-for participants to get together on another pretext—for dinner, to dance, or to listen to music—mentioning that some of the group might engage in party sex, and warning anyone who might be offended to decline the invitation (and planting the seed of curiosity early in the others).

The hosts must make it clear that no one will be under any pressure to participate. The initiators should then hold back for an hour or two so that they don't scare the neophytes as their curiosity grows. In many cases desire will overcome fear, and the inexperienced are apt to make the first advances.

The whole group might play recordings of their favorite popular music and dance their favorite dance, or one or two talented members might be chosen to dance while the others watch. If there is time and an interest in the Tantric ceremony, the group might ask a member who is more familiar with the single couple ritual, someone who is open and serenely at home with his sexual nature, to perform it with his partner first while the others look on. Their calm arousal should catch and inspire the others, helping them to focus their libido.

The celebrants may meditate silently or read the invocation of Shiva and Parvati from the *Ananga Ranga* to set a reverent mood.

> May you be purified by Parvati, who colored the nails of her hands, which were white as the waters of the Ganges, with lac after seeing the fire on the forehead of Shiva: Who painted her eyes with color after seeing the dark hues of Shiva's neck and whose body-hair stood erect with desire after seeing in a mirror the ashes on Shiva's body.
>
> I invoke thee, O Kamadeva! [The God of love.] Thee the sportive; Thee the wanton one, who dwellest in the hearts of all created beings; Thou instillest courage . . . Thou sufficest unto Rati, and to the loves and pleasures of the world!

Thou art ever cheerful, removing uneasiness and overactivity, and thou givest comfort and happiness to the mind of man.*

Like the single couple ritual, the group sex ritual for worship should begin with the Shiva marriage of the participants. The men and women both must look upon their partners as embodiments of the male or female creative principle.

After the preliminary activities, such as burning incense, singing and dancing, the start of the actual ritual for most Indian sects is signaled by the sounding of the mystic syllable *Om*, which is said to contain all sound, and represents cosmic energy. Repeating *Om* helps clear the mind of outside preoccupations. In India the partners rinse their mouths and feet with water and bathe a stone lingam. They walk around the phallic symbol and prostrate themselves or genuflect before it. Finding a suitable stone lingam in the West is difficult, so I suggest that the actual male organ be venerated in such a manner by the females, with an equal exchange on the part of the males in reverence for the yoni. The partners can take turns and will have to genuflect or perform deep reverence. Worshiping the real thing rather than a cold stone substitute is much more fun for both parties, it seems to me, and all lingams are manifestations of the Great Lingam. While worshiping the lingam, one can keep in mind actual words from the cult of Shiva. "Shiva, I worship thy image whose form is radiant as a mountain of silver, lovely as the crescent of the moon and resplendent with jewels." In Buddhist texts it is called the "lightning-jewel."

Remember that to the Hindu temple builders nothing that was natural was obscene. They accepted life as they saw it.

The details of the ritual are basically the same as outlined in Chapter 2. A little wine, "the great medicine for humanity, which maketh glad the heart of man, helping it to forget deep sorrows," is drunk. Then fish, meat and grain are eaten to communicate with all life in symbolic union. Finally the actual maithuna is enjoyed, "which is the cause of intense pleasure, the origin of all breathing creatures, and the root of the world."

To avoid repetition, I will only stress that there must be enough light for the celebrants to be able to see each other, and that they should proceed in an unhurried and unembarrassed manner. They should feel physically and spiritually pure at the termination of the ritual. If for any reason—perhaps the fear of

* *Ananga Ranga*, translated by Sir Richard Burton for the Kama Shastra Society of London, 1885. Library of Congress.

the new and the unknown—the ritual fails to satisfy any of the participants they should not worry, but hope to have the chance to participate again. The realm of *ek-stasis*, where the individual lets go and reaches outside himself and his normal role, is worth an effort.

If you get carried away and forget the format of the ritual nothing is lost; on the contrary. The format is only a guide. As Vatsyayana pointed out so long ago, spontaneous congress is best. "If one has more than middling passion no form is necessary when the wheels of love take over."

The Tantric ritual avoids some of the disadvantages of the American version of group sex, swinging, where I have heard that an orifice, any orifice, will do. During the preliminaries experimentation is encouraged, but afterward not just any orifice will do: the yoni should be filled. There is no abrupt changing of partners; if done, this is gently done, usually around a circle so there are no piles of sweaty, heaving, ejaculating bodies. There is great concern for beauty. The mind and spirit are brought into play as well as the body, for there is psychological as well as physical contact. In the group ritual as in the single couple ritual, the partner is highly cherished as a god or goddess, even though the couple may not see each other again. This mitigates against the defect in the usual American practice of group sex, described by anthropologist Charles Bartell in a recent book called *Group Sex*. Bartell believes that "the total non-involvement in partners whom they may never see again represents the antithesis of sexual pleasure, and even contributes to a feeling of depersonalization."

While I have heard and read about Tantric group rituals and been told about and researched the American practice, I have tried neither. Those who have will have to substantiate these comments coming from indirect experience; and I hope they will make their own variations on the liturgy.

10 Sexual Stories—Games and Play

Long ago the Indians recognized and developed sex as play as well as reverence. In their daily lives there is little stuffy separation of one from the other. I learned about most of these games while visiting two harems in Rajasthan, but they are not exclusively harem games, since most of them were played long before there were harems in India.

The legend of the young god Krishna and the gopis is the basic inspiration for many of these games. Several long poems illustrated with miniature paintings from Kangra, such as the *Gita Govinda* and the *Bhagavata Purana*, develop the central theme of the Krishna cult, which is the yearning for, the seeking, and finally the experience of self-loss in finding a higher reality. The gopis, beautiful young cow girls from Brindaban, left their homes, their families, responsibilities, personas and roles to wander in the dark forest, afraid and vulnerable, in search of this feeling, symbolized by Krishna. But the Tantric goal of self-loss, even momentary, is frightening. The spontaneous, childlike excitement that builds up in the games makes the loss of limiting controls more likely to take us unawares. A transcendent experience may happen here more easily at first than in the ritual, where one is determined to melt away and may become too self-conscious. If you're not mystically inclined by nature, you may prefer to start to forget yourself and all your burdens first in games where action helps to carry you away. If you stumble upon cosmic consciousness first in sexual games, you may want to try for the same experience voluntarily in the full relaxation of the sexual ritual.

In games you can dress up and mask yourself to be someone

else, whomever you choose; whoop and holler; stretch your muscles in kinetic joy to make your blood boil. Sex-play arouses childlike peaks of overall excitement and tension, leading to a climax reserved for adults.

The wilder games allow many people to release quite a bit of violence and fear, running and shrieking it out, leaving deadening armor far behind.

Rape and bondage games help lead to sexual release both by building tension and by overcoming old anxieties, as sometimes people can more easily permit the let-go of orgasm when it is forced upon them. If you are daring, try these games under the noonday sun in country fields, in cool dark forests, along river banks, and at night in parks, on golf courses, or in a suburban yard. Or you can try them at home or just in your head.

PANTY RAID   The most epic panty raid remembered in history or legend occurred like this, according to the *Bhagavata Purana*: One January the gopis of Nanda kept a fast in honor of their chosen goddess, eating only what was left of sacrificial offerings. They went to the banks of the Jamuna to make a sand image of the goddess to worship and, tempted by the water, took off their clothes, entered the water, and began to play. Krishna and his companions were nearby, grazing cows, when they heard the gopis singing. When he saw the charming scene a prank came into Krishna's mind. He gathered up their clothes and climbed a large tree, joking and laughing with the other boys.

When the refreshed gopis finished splashing, bathing and sporting, they noticed there were no clothes on the bank. Alarmed, they looked about on the ground and wondered to each other who could have taken their clothes.

At last one of the girls spotted Krishna in the tree, wearing a necklace of flowers.

"There he is, friends, the stealer of our hearts, the stealer of our clothes, sitting in the kadamba tree, holding a bundle."

Knowing Krishna could see them, they felt ashamed at their nakedness and entered the water, pleading, "Compassionate to the humble, beloved remover of grief, O Mohan, please give us our clothes. Why are you deceiving us, Darling of Nanda! We are plain simple girls. A trick has been played; our consciousness and sense are gone; you have played this prank, O Hari!"

Hearing them, Krishna said, "I will not give like this. Come

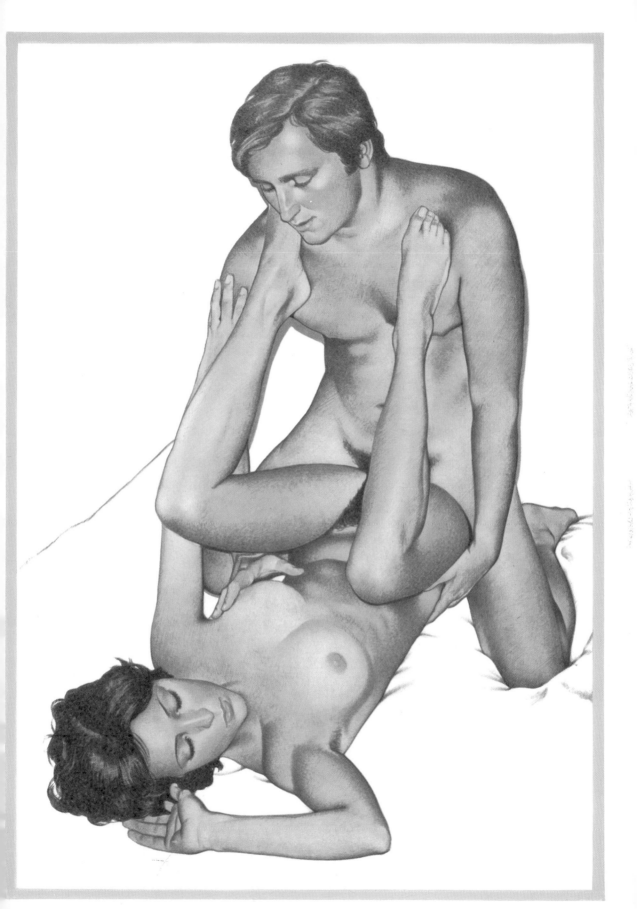

AVIDARITA ASANA

SPHUTMA BANDHA

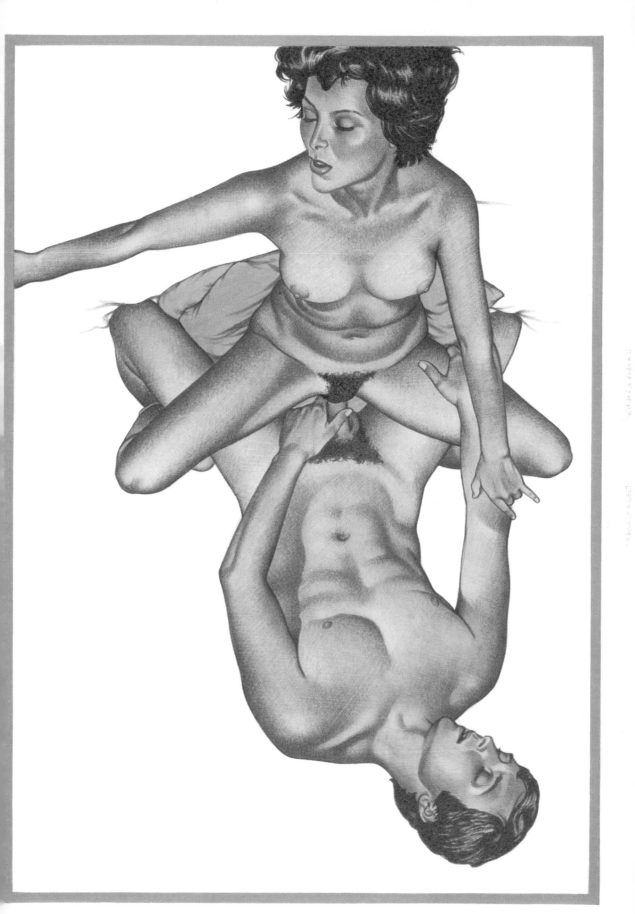

JRIMBHITA ASANA

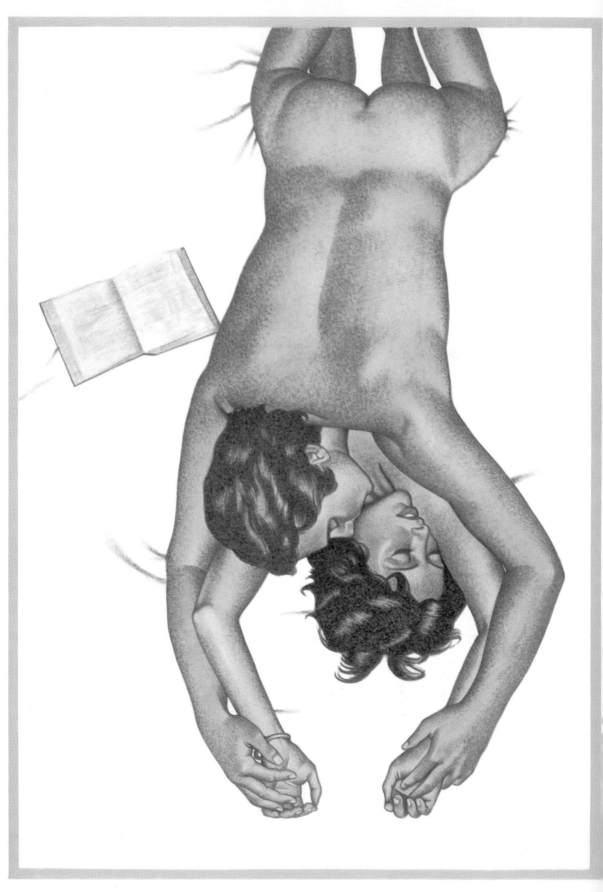

PUHAPAKA ASANA

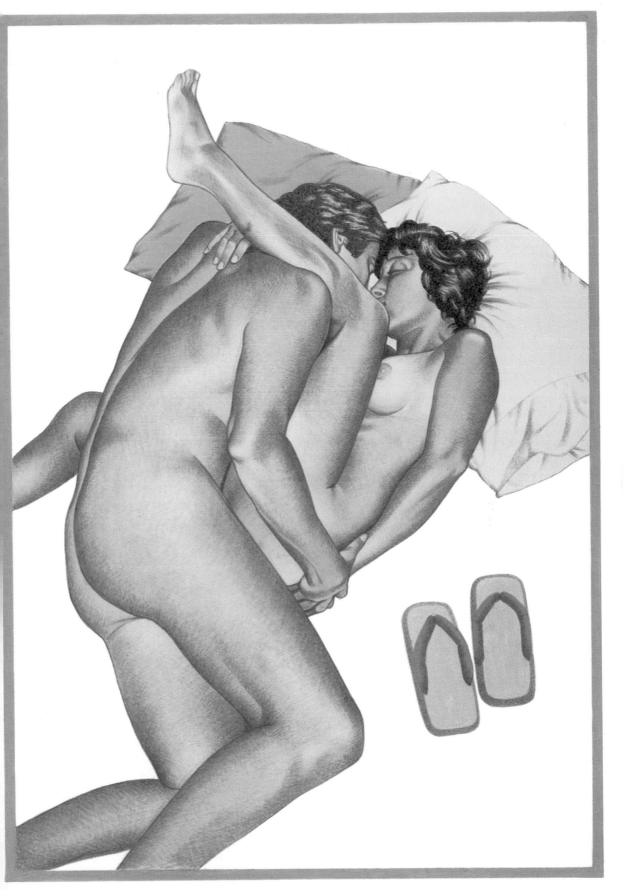

LATA ASANA

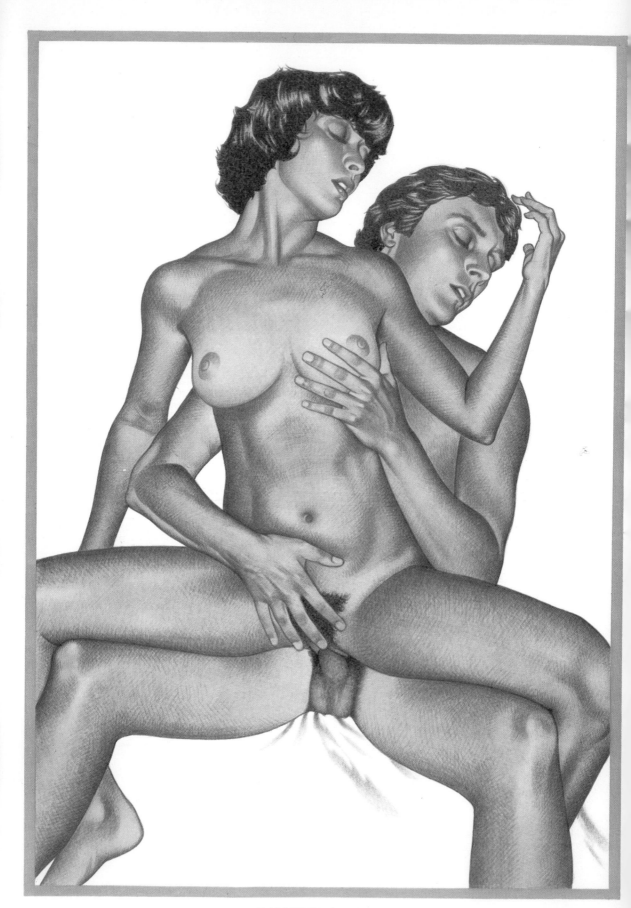

CANCHALA ASANA

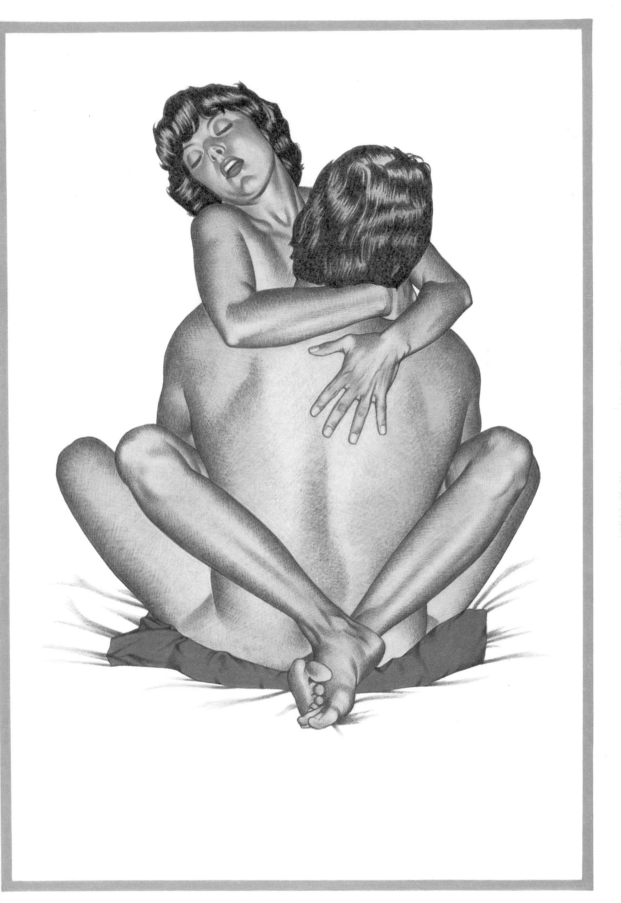

SUHAPADMA ASANA

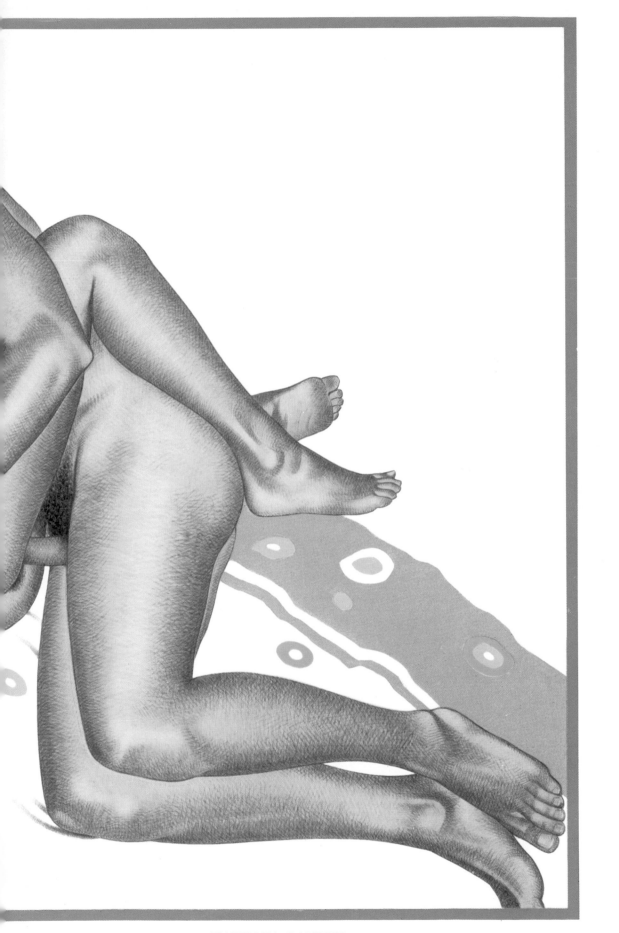

KARKATA BANDHA

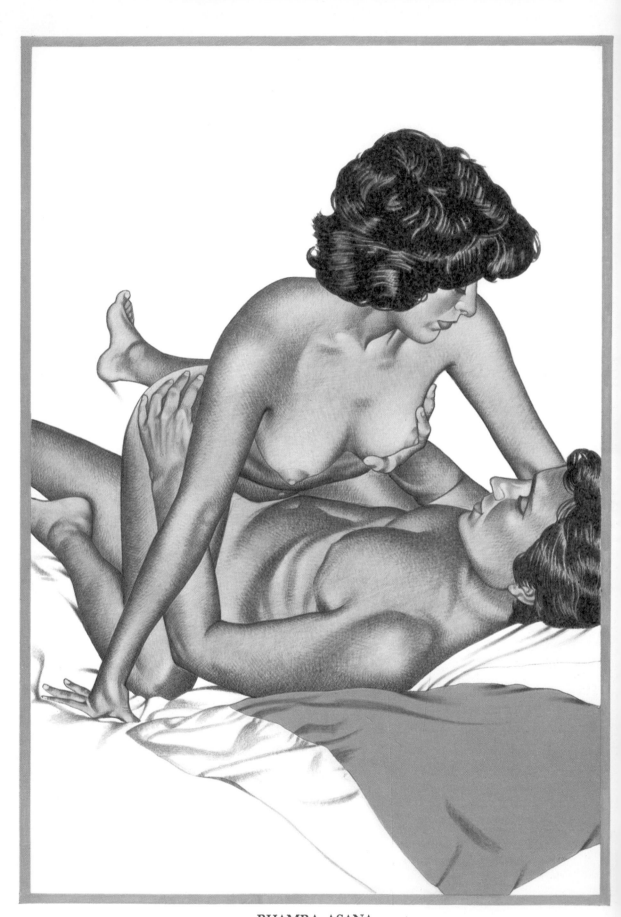

BHAMRA ASANA

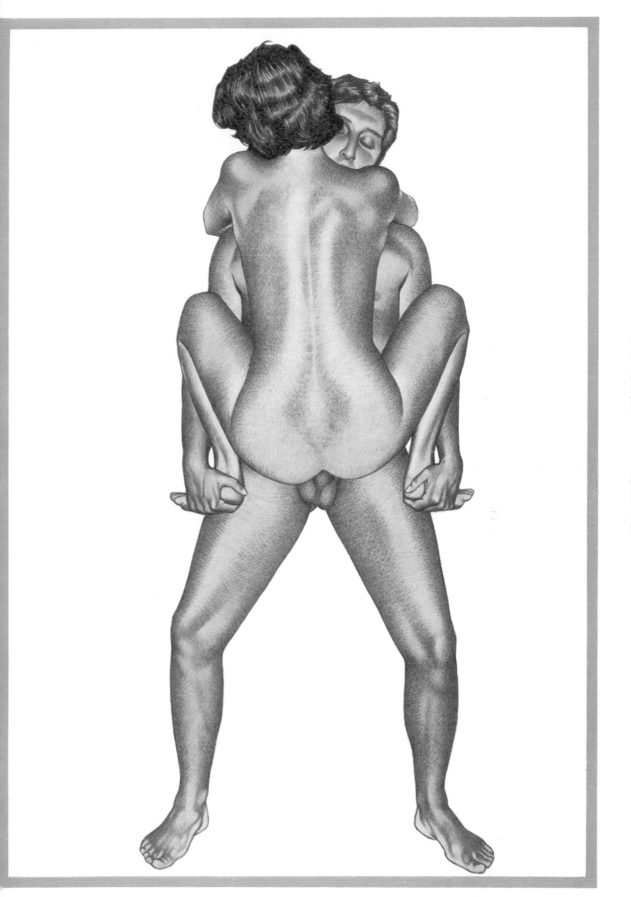

YONI ASANA

VAIDHURIT ASANA

out one by one, with joined hands, then you will receive your clothes."

After talking it over among themselves, the gopis decided: "Come, friends! What Mohan says we should respect; he knows the state of our body and mind; what shame is there in this?"

Feeling helpless and shy, the girls came out one by one, with bowed heads and joined hands, to receive their clothes.

Pleased with the purity of their hearts, Krishna spoke to them and invited them to come back another time to sport with him.*

American students have long made variations on this ancient game. Try your own and end them however you prefer.

GO FISH   For a group wanting a more sexual game, this variation on the clothing game imitates the Kaulas and other sects in Bengal who had the women in the group put their choli tops into a pile for the men to draw, in order to choose their sex partners at random. Keys, shoes and men's belts all work as well. Here in the words of a nineteenth-century visitor to India, Horace Wilson, is the promiscuity rite of the Kanchuliyas. "[This sect] is said to be distinguished by one peculiar rite, the object of which is to confound all the ties of female alliance, and to enforce not only a community of women among the votaries, but disregard even to natural restraints. On occasions of worship the female votaries are said to deposit their vests [or cholis, which serve both as blouse and bra] in a box in charge of the Guru. At the close of the usual rites the male worshippers take each a vest from the box and the female to whom the garment appertains, be she ever so nearly of kin to him, is the partner for the time in his licentious pleasures."†

WATER GAMES   Later in the parable of Krishna and the gopis, the maidens, with beautiful faces surrounded by curls and wreathed in smiles of sweetest nectar, sang the glorious deeds of the supreme one, thrilled by the touch of his fingernails.

With flower garlands crushed from contact with their limbs

---

* Adapted from M. S. Randhawa, *Kangra Paintings of the Bhagavata Purana* (New Delhi; National Museum of India, 1960), p. 62.

† Horace H. Wilson, as quoted by George Ryley Scott in *Phallic Worship*. London; Panther Books, 1970, p. 183.

and illuminated by the red powder from their bosoms, followed by swarms of bumblebees, tired Krishna entered the water like a tusker followed by female elephants.

"Oh, my love!" the girls laughed lovingly as they splashed him here and there with water in fun. He was adored by the celestials from their vehicles as they rained flowers on him; and he, delighting in his own supreme self, enjoyed himself in sport.

Then Krishna and the bevy of girls, like a male elephant in rut with his female elephants, moved into the garden along the river, laden with the breeze-blown perfume of flowers. The swarm of bumblebees followed the Lord like singing angels.*

As you read, imagine the beautiful wet look of lightly clothed bodies playing in the water, so often shown in Kangra miniature paintings.

Water games are a good setting to try some of the athletic positions in which the man stands and holds the woman up and she winds her arms and legs around him like a creeping vine. Bodies weigh so much less, and merge and change positions easily and gracefully.

Because of increased mobility and reduced friction, water may be the best place to try anal sex for the first time.

BODY PAINTING   In the words of a later poet, Jayadeva, this is the way Radha spoke to Krishna after a night of love with him in a forest bower, as she prepared to dress before the company of gopis could see her confusion.

> With fingers cooler than sandal-wood, paint, O Krishna, leaves and flowers of musk on this breast, which resembles a vase of consecrated water, crowned with fresh leaves near a green bower to propitiate the God of Love. Hang on my ears the jewelled earrings, O accomplished youth, and let the antelopes of thine eyes run down to remember our sporting at pleasure. Arrange my tresses, O beloved Krishna, round my temples. O Love, now place a fresh circle of musk, black as the lunar spots, on the moon of my forehead; and mix gay flowers in my tresses with a peacock's feathers, that they may wave gracefully like the banners of Kama.
>
> While she spoke, Krishna obeyed her playful requests, and placed musky spots on her bosom and forehead, dyed her temples with radiant hues, embellished her eyes with dark kohl, decked

---

* Adapted from M. S. Randhawa, *op. cit.*, p. 72.

her braided hair and her neck with fresh garlands and tied brace-
lets on her wrists, rings on her ankles and around her waist the
zone of bells that sounded with ravishing melody.*

Passionately helping each other undress and tenderly to dress
is a more simplified version for all lovers.

Bathing each other is also great fun. Sit in the tub, one in front
of the other, and soap each other. Play with each other's slippery
feet as if catching elusive fish in your hands. Make swirls of
soapy foam all over each other's bodies and in each other's pubic
hair; then dry each other off.

MOCK RAPE Many cultures have versions of this game, which often takes
place just after a wedding ceremony, perhaps because it is so
exciting and so much fun for both the participants and the
vicariously aroused onlookers. Mock rape leaves no time for
everyday preoccupations.

The man chases the woman at full speed, catches her, gasping,
and flings her over his shoulder, then throws her down. He opens
her legs as wide as he can or puts her ankles over her head so that
she feels completely helpless and dominated by him. Then he
takes her, pumping furiously (as long as he knows the squeals
are in pleasure and surprise, not pain).

Or (if she likes bondage games) he can tie her to the bedposts
or feet-together with knees opened wide for their mutual pleasure. When she ties him it may increase his excitement and ability
to surrender. Muscle tension as he strains against the bonds can
also make for a more all-over orgasm rather than a localized one.

AMBUSH This simplified form of the many rape game variations can be
played any time she (or he) comes in the door for dinner, to
listen to music, or just returning home. Put dinner in the oven
and ambush her at the door, pushing her down on the living
room floor for the most satisfying first course in the world. If you
live together, attack any time before your usual bedtime when
she is not quite expecting it, preferably not in the bedroom.
Scoop her up and carry her to a new place.

* *Ibid.*, pp. 104–110.

THE PILLOW GAME   This was played in many harems in Rajasthan, perhaps to give a harem woman a chance to be the boss, at least for an hour.

A couple undresses and each takes a small down-filled pillow which has been opened at one end. The point of the game is to beat each other with the pillows until there are no feathers left in the cases. The first to empty all the feathers wins, getting the right to be the "lord" for the hour.

The pillow game is played with furious frenzy, each opponent beating the other on the breasts, the head, the legs, the thighs, buttocks, anywhere but the face, until the room is so filled with feathers the lovers can hardly see each other, but must tell where to continue hitting by the laughing, snorting and heavy breathing.

The winner can choose his or her favorite position or positions. If she wins she can ride him like a horse or elephant, then turn him to ride in the Shakti on Shiva asana. He may prefer, if he has won the right to be "lord," to have her bend down on all fours in a wild pile of feathers. Later, the loser must pick up all the feathers and restuff the pillows for the next battle.

BREAK PLUM   A game of sharing fruit, Break Plum is much more intimate than breaking bread and is loved by Indians and visitors to India who have tried it. The friend who told me about it is a well-known writer and Sanskrit scholar who explored India and the Tantras after graduation from Columbia University thirty years ago.

During love-play the woman takes a large, firm, succulent plum, slits one side of it, and carefully extracts the seed. She pulls it apart far enough to fit on the end of the man's erect penis, licking off any juice that begins to trickle down. Wearing this purple cap, the man plays with his partner as he will, until they are ready for penetration. The large plum may give a small man a more heroic self-image to keep in his heart, and gives the woman added sensation during his passion strokes.

Finally the plum will come off deep inside her. Now he must retrieve the crushed plum by sucking and using his tongue. If he needs to use his fingers he loses and must play again or forfeit to her. If she wants, she can help squeeze the plum out by squatting and pushing. When the juicy prize is retrieved, they break it in half and eat it, before he goes back inside the fragrant vagina to produce his own nectar. If you can't find a succulent plum you can use a small ripe peach, a large apricot, or even some of the whole canned fruits such as spiced apples and peaches, which will make up in juiciness what they lack in firmness.

DELAYS AND TEASING   The one sexual principle or bit of knowledge that a fifteen-year-old virgin was taught before she was sent by the maharaja to entertain a visitor was to delay the man's entry until she had had an orgasm. This is charming in itself, my friend tells me, and ensures that her first intercourse will be well lubricated and pleasurable, even if there is blood. There is an element of challenge to both partners to heighten the initial excitement and use the most satisfying techniques of foreplay. After the first orgasm he can try to give her another using combinations of short shallow strokes, to make sure he does not hurt her, and then long deep strokes before they share an orgasm together.

Other ways to delay which I've seen in miniature paintings include listening to music, playing cards, or even practicing archery for the lovers to show off their control while they are linked, the woman using just enough constriction to help him stay hard until they are ready to come, perhaps an hour later.

Another method of delay is simply a matter of one partner pushing the other on to orgasm while he or she holds back to delay, and enjoys the getting there as long as possible. Some people say they think of the multiplication tables. This can be done with bondage and slow masturbation, which few people can stand if they are not tied down.

For a different sort of tease, have the working partner build up and stop just before orgasm again and again until the subject mews and begs to be finished off. See how berserk you can drive your partner. Delay makes the orgasm more intense, as the dammed-up tension finally breaks loose.

Or see how many orgasmic peaks you can make him or her scale.

Imaginative couples can make sex games from many of the old favorite childhood games: follow the leader, drop the handkerchief and Marco Polo, among others.

MOTION GAMES   The Lake Palace in Udaipur, now a hotel, has a suite equipped with an elegant swing almost as big as a bed, hanging over a thick carpet. The broad, cushioned seat is covered in bright embroidery

Swings   and mirror work. Four brass chains hold it to the ceiling, every other link cast in the form of a voluptuous wide-hipped woman, an elephant or a large-beaked bird. Besides the huge bed and the stained glass in the tops of the windows, which makes changing fretwork patterns of color on the white floor, the swing is the crowning feature of the room and looks out over the lake through arched windows.

This is the closest thing the ancients had to a water bed, giving an unstable, bouncy feeling that both partners can enjoy, and that makes the slimmest courtesan or wife underneath feel like a jiggly fat earth mother with neverending flesh. (You'll know what I mean if you saw the scene in *Satyricon* where the young hero gets back his potency.)

Fragonard painted suggestions and the movies show us fade-outs, at least, of the erotic possibilities of sex on a high-speed swing, with its rise and downward pull, then the weightlessness as it falls, followed by another stronger pull as it rises again—changes in pressure that produce unusual and wonderful sensations in the pelvis.

When you swing united, the woman astride the man's lap in the Yoni asana, pumping up the swing will carry your congress until the momentum you build up is enough to carry you on. Then you let the peak die down gently.

Use the children's or let the neighbors wonder why you have hung an extra-sturdy swing in the garden now that the children are gone.

Elephant Back   The young sons of a well-known maharaja (and perhaps the father in his day) used to seduce their girl friends on the back of the family elephant—a more exotic location than the usual car seat. Sometimes at sunset they would seat the girl ahead of them on the painted and decorated elephant, which they headed into the familiar climb to the high fortress palace, with the girl rocking and falling back against them. At times the girl would pretend to ignore the rubbing, but sometimes turned around to cooperate for a unique feeling during intercourse, letting the even rolling and rocking of the seat on the elephant's back produce all the movement needed for a satisfying and different congress. This is quite unlike the lurching of a camel, which would give its own distinct sensation. Camels are also common in Rajasthan, but anyone can try a rocking chair for a homey substitute.

Horseback Riding   If you don't have access to a real steed you can trust, you can use your imaginations and mount each other for the fun of it. Secretariat is well nicknamed "Sexy," for horses are sexy, especially spirited ones to adolescent girls. Just the sight and smell and naturalness of beautiful animals can have an erotic effect on some people. And the feel of the animal's power and rippling muscles is quite a turn-on, as are the thrill and rhythm of the free motion of a canter or gallop. Both sexes can identify with a stallion's single-minded interest in a mare in season to the point of almost berserk excitement.

Most of my Indian friends had beautifully trained polo ponies that could be ridden for romantic purposes. If you can get a reliable horse, gallop together to a secluded spot, letting desire and abandon build, then he can leap off and lift her down to the ground.

Or ride together on the same horse in the moonlight—if the man has good balance and legs, and if you can trust your horse—as a preliminary, for the rubbing and close movement, or even united for a unique feeling.

Try a rocking horse left over from childhood—the man facing forward while the woman faces him.

Small Boats   The most romantic small boat I've found, now that the canals of Venice have become sewers, is the shikara of Kashmir. This gracefully curved and pointed gondola has a large, canopy-covered and curtained seat decorated with bold designs in bright gold and red. Shrinagar abounds in clear lakes and canals to be explored at sunrise or sunset, fed by melting snows from the backdrop of mighty young Himalayas and lesser mountains in the foreground, surrounding the valley. The shallowness of the craft and the nearness to every wave in the water give passengers a swimmy feeling that's quite unreal. Gliding along with eight or ten other shikaras may be the closest some tourists ever get to group sex. Any movement you make is amplified by the reaction of the water.

In a pinch, a raft, a rowboat with a removable seat, a small sailboat, or a yacht will do, but the larger the craft, the less actual feel of the water you have.

Trains   Love on a speeding train contrasts with the unhurried gentleness and quiet love in a shikara, where the only sound is of an oar dipped in water. Here there is a reeling and constant clacking to remind you of speeding movement and a sense of urgency as the whistle calls. The closeness of a small confined space adds intimacy in a compartment. If you're behind a curtain only, the turn-on of knowing other people are near and passing can add extra excitement. Everything carries you away from the ordinary.

11 Lifelong Potency for the Aging Worshiper

TANTRA IS UNIQUE AMONG mystical schools in its concern for the welfare of the body. The body is seen as the vessel of consciousness, not its enemy. Tantrics believe that their school of yoga, called Kundalini yoga, conserves health and delays aging by concentrating on the body's symbolic sex center, the Muladhara. Regular stimulation of this symbolic sex center awakens a source of quiescent energy, postponing aging.

Today the study of hormones shows that sexual stimulation does help to keep the body younger. But the benefit of sex is more than just a matter of hormones. Pleasure is vital to health. Pleasure is expansion, the moving out from the self into the world of joy. Pain is contraction, a shutting-in. The greatest source of pleasure is the full sexual orgasm. Notice how closely the orgasmic cycle approximates the life cycle in cell reproduction: tension—charge—discharge—relaxation.

Tantra also teaches that human sex in itself is no different from animal sex; to obtain full benefit there must be love too. The mind and emotions must be involved during the sex rituals. In fact, the sex partners must regard each other as gods and goddesses, thus building into the ritual an attitude of reverence and devotion. The psychological benefits of loving follow: a rekindling of enthusiasm, spontaneity, freshness and the wonder of youth.

Tantra outlines an excellent program to preserve health: a light natural diet, loose clothing, exercise, deep breathing, relaxation, not too much sun, and the sex ritual regularly. Tantrics avoid today's Jockey shorts and tight-fitting pants for men because these hold in excessive body heat, which reduces the production of sperm by the testes.

Tantrics also teach the power of positive thinking. They call it *Shiwa*, or the doctrine of magical power. Shiwa, an ancient form of mind control, prevents misfortunes, guards against illness, and is used to prolong life. Today we know that fulfillment and happiness are therapeutic. Buoyant personalities are much less likely to succumb to cancer, according to a recent study. We also know that many body functions long considered automatic can be modified. The power of auto-suggestion helps the Tantric yogi to stay vital, since he believes that during the practice of his disciplines, including the sex ritual, he sucks in extra doses of cosmic energy.

But the Path of Pleasure is not just a romp in the hay. For those who follow it, Tantra requires intelligence, discipline, perseverance, mental control, attention to detail, and balance. All these are habits that become more important as we grow older.

Our expectations, and those society holds for us, tend to become self-fulfilling prophecies. To a great extent, our self-image and mental health depend on the acceptance and support of the group, so we are often ruled by "what people might say."

In our culture, a "dirty old man" is an object of disgust and ridicule. A dirty old woman is so unthinkable the expression is not even used. Usually the psychic castration that begins when she is just a little girl and is told that it is bad to "play with yourself" is enough to squash the sexuality in a woman long before she is old. If desire lasts, it may bring shame and guilt.

In our obsession with youth we overlook the needs of aging men and women for sexual comfort. While most of us will be happy to accept a long old age and to plan for it when we consider the alternative (death), how much more readily we might accept age if we could look forward to—indeed count upon—continued sexual fulfillment.

Even Eastern cultures have been ignorant about sex in the later years and share Western society's present stereotype—a sexless old age. There are a number of noxious myths and misconceptions that are held the world over. The first and oldest is that the loss of semen will diminish the body's vital force. The ancient Chinese believed that *yang*, or semen, was limited, and that if ejaculation were restrained the vital semen would rise to the brain. The famous Greek physician Galen wrote, "In emissions of semen, we lose the vital force; it is not surprising that too frequent coition enervates, since it deprives the body of its purest parts."*

These old attitudes are wrong, wrong, wrong. In *Sexual Life After Sixty*, Dr. Isadore Rubin points out that the basis of these beliefs has been swept away by modern scientific knowledge. "Today it is well recognized that the emission of semen is no more of a loss than is the expectoration of saliva. Both semen and saliva are quickly replaced by the body." Nevertheless, these old myths occasionally reappear in print and in the regimens of athletic teams, such as the Russians, who are required to be continent before games.

Another error is the idea that one can prolong sex life by being inactive in the earlier years and less active in the later years, as if there were only so many comes in a person. However, the Kinsey investigators found that people who were most active in their earlier lives were also the most active in later years. Regular activity is now known to be the best way to secure the longest possible functioning of *all* parts of the body, as anyone knows who has ever spent a week in bed (alone). "Use it or lose it," modern doctors say.

In actual practice, individual activity and attitudes vary widely. The philosopher Arthur Schopenhauer no doubt summed up the point of view of many older men when he declared that he was grateful to old age because it brought release from "a monster tyrant: sex." Behind this idea of sex as a tyrant lies the strong implicit rejection, conscious or unconscious, of sex in the earlier years. Often age may be used as an excuse to end a function tainted with anxiety.

Even Sigmund Freud, the great spokesman of the importance of sex, in his later years didn't practice what he preached. He wrote that in his fifties he was surprised to find that he could, on *one* occasion, feel physically attracted to a young woman! This contrasts sharply with the diary of Victor Hugo, who noted just three months before his death at the age of eighty-three that he had had sexual relations eight times during the past year.

One of my Tantric friends is a French mathematician engaged in operational research. He told me his work has improved in the

---

* Orthodox Buddhist Tantrics train themselves to ejaculate into the bladder, thinking they are conserving semen, or bindu. (Not all Tantrics knew everything about sex two thousand years ago.) However, the Hindu left-hand path teaches healthy fulfillment in full orgasm.

last two years, in spite of the fact that he is over sixty, since he incorporated Tantric ideas into his life and started practicing the sexual ritual. "Since I began meditating and cultivating my sexual powers my mental powers seem to have increased as well. By enlarging my capacity for carnal pleasure my capacity for work seems to have increased, too. During sex I feel an emotional link with the rest of the world that I seem to draw on when I work with abstractions for long periods of time."

Modern authorities now agree on the sexual prognosis for both men and women over forty, fifty, or seventy: excellent. Live sperm has been found in men over ninety. There are reliable accounts of men who became fathers in their seventies, eighties and nineties.

In the past we have been told to age gracefully. "Fight age" is the new motto. We see that the acceptance of old age holds out little if any reward. Upon analyzing lengthy interviews with 600 aged San Franciscans, anthropologist Margaret Clark found that engagement with life, rather than detachment, contributed most to psychological well-being.

Those who surrender to old age often do so because they believe in a debilitating mystique of age. Studies at the University of Illinois of 900 old people living at home found many so sick that they could not walk to the door. They had lived for months without medical attention because they felt they were old and therefore supposed to be sick. If sickness is often accepted as an inevitable part of aging, how much more often is sexlessness expected and accepted?

A couple in their sixties went for treatment to the Reproductive Research Foundation of Masters and Johnson in St. Louis. They had lived unhappily with the husband's impotence for five years. Prior to that period, the couple had enjoyed sex for many years. Then the husband noticed that getting an erection took longer. When this happened a few times, his concern changed to panic and he became impotent. Several doctors told them that the husband's condition was a natural result of aging and that they should learn to accept it. Finally one doctor referred them to the Foundation. After two weeks of therapy they resumed an active sex life.

Even long-term sex problems in people over forty have been cured at the Foundation's clinic. Just two weeks of treatment at the clinic, combining behavior therapy with physical instruction and experimentation, can change lives. Women who were non-orgasmic for over fifty years have at last achieved climax. The longer the problem has been in existence, however, the harder it is to reverse, and the success rates go down from eighty percent cured for patients in general to about two-thirds cured in the upper age bracket.

The experience of my Tantric friends who practice the sex rituals indefinitely is confirmed by Dr. Masters' studies of the sexual responses of the aging. In his view the studies of sexual performance in aging people are far more significant and radical than the sexual revolution among today's youth, and will affect more people directly than anything else in *Human Sexual Inadequacy*, once they are disseminated.

Attitudes based on the Path of Pleasure can help many people convert dramatically to the acceptance and use of their bodies.

Sexual joy can provide an important form of ego reinforcement through the feeling of being needed and loved at a time when other satisfactions are being withdrawn. Sex can provide comfort during an identity crisis caused by retirement or the empty nest. The exchange of warmth, pleasure and affection is even more precious now because of the increasing sense of isolation and anxiety. Sex is an antidote for the loneliness of the nuclear family and the dangers of over-civilization. It links us with our instincts, releases our tension, is a gentle balm and a potent energizer.

The process of sexual aging is as much a mystery as the process of aging per se. We do know that cell division begins to slow down with age and there is a failure in the body's self-governing mechanism. Yet Tantra's theories about the release and re-absorption of energy during the sexual ritual offer one explanation for the youthful appearance of almost all its disciples.

Sexual response is complex at any age. Arousal involves the whole personality rather than just the body. By the time the sex organs mature they are already under the dominance of psychological, social and cultural factors which can block the spontaneous sexual process. Habits, childhood memories, old scars, daily pressures, all can interfere.

As one ages it is important to know that there are two kinds of erections. The first comes from mental stimuli and is common in boys and young men. But, with the exception of trained yogis in the East and some sexy men in the West, the powers of mental erection tend to become extinct as men age. The second is a tactile or reflex erection from touching of the sex organ. This type of erection persists. Because of this, the female partner should take a more active, tactile role during arousal with an older man. However, the Tantric practice of meditation and mind control can keep the powers of psychic arousal alive and vigorous.

One reason for the terror of growing old in America is our concept of sexual allure. Bound by ignorance and stereotypes, many people consider only the young and beautiful to be sexually desirable. The problem is a dual one because it involves our self-image as well as the way we see our partner. We may not consider ourselves desirable after a certain age, whether it be forty, fifty, or sixty. Chateaubriand, the great French author, wrote that he could not believe that a young woman could love him and want him sexually when he was old—and even if she could, he could not allow it!

The problem of desirability may well be a real one. Many people allow a physical and emotional erosion to take place as they age, leaving them with little attraction. But this is not inevitable. Examples abound of "ugly" people who are attractive and "old" men and women who are still glamorous and beautiful.

Doctors' claims that the small decline in male hormones in most older men should not hinder their sex lives indicate that we must look for other causes of limited sexuality in aging men and women in our society. These limiting factors are the harmful attitudes that have been mentioned and the pressures of daily life, for the most part.

Certain changes occur in the sex organs after fifty or sixty, although there is a great deal of individual variation. The testicles become smaller and less firm. The membranes in the tubes that produce sperm become thickened. The blood vessels degenerate a bit, and sperm production declines; but unless there is some disease, accident, or operation, production of sperm does not cease *at any time*.

Aging does not begin at forty, as many people think. In fact, sexual aging in the male begins with adolescence. Although there are individual variations, the decline in male sexuality is remarkably steady from even the early and middle teens.

But nature is over-generous in youth, so the fact that there is a decline in both hormones and vigor does not in any way mean that a very rewarding sexual life cannot be continued, resumed, or even begun in later life. The important thing is *joie de vivre*, not olympic performances.

Certain changes do take place in the sexual response cycle. In fact, all body processes change with age, but, with the exception of sex, they are not expected to stop.

The first of the four phases in the sexual cycle, the excitement phase, when erection takes place, does take longer. Without constant practice of the yoga of sex, the older man will be far less likely to get an erection in response to visual or mental stimuli alone than he was when he was younger. He will generally need to be touched or sucked. The erection may not be as hard at first as it used to be. Men first experiencing this slowdown often panic because our society, like most cultures, has conditioned them to see it as the beginning of the end of sexual ability. As Dr. Masters puts it, "When a man notices his erective slowdown he usually thinks, 'Oh God, it's gone and there is nothing I can do about it' and so he worries and doesn't have an erection."

The fear of failing may actually cause failure; fear can block response. Many, many men give up trying altogether.

The potential for erection remains unchanged, however, and the loss is only secondary. *Sexology* Magazine quizzed a group of older men who answered that involuntary morning erections continue five or ten years longer after the onset of impotence. (Think of the waste!)

Teeth-gritting willpower cannot help a man to get an erection. Sexual response is a natural process that may become inhibited in an atmosphere of preoccupation and effort. Trying too hard brings comparable results in the golf swing and the act of love. Once a person begins to watch his own sexual responses in a "spectator role" instead of getting involved naturally, the sexual stimuli are apt to be blocked. I know that certain yogis in India can produce erections at will and actually lift weights with their male members, but this is exceptional.

If a person is trying to prove how virile, how good a lover he is, there may be problems. Far better to relax and think of how much "we" can enjoy together.

There are more changes in the aging male's orgasmic phase. Instead of the two-stage ejaculatory phase that is common in young men, there may be no inevitability stage—that period of sharp urgency when a man feels he can no longer hold back and must come. After fifty, there may be only the expulsion stage, when the jet of semen is expelled from the penis; or the inevitability stage may be shortened by half (from seven to three or four seconds).

An older man comes with less force, especially if the testes fail to elevate, as sometimes happens, and there is not as much seminal fluid. But as long as the man does not worry about this it will not deprive him or his partner of enjoyment.

The resolution phase is much shorter than before, the penis

becoming soft within seconds after ejaculation. A man who might have been able to have another erection within minutes when younger may now have to wait for hours.

Masters and Johnson stress that there is less demand for an older man to ejaculate, and that he should do so only when he really wants to. Because of the popular idea of intercourse, both partners usually feel they have failed if the man does not come. This attitude can be harmful if the couple tries to force ejaculation. Sexual needs and tastes vary from person to person and should be met accordingly to avoid a sense of failure. In later life this principle is most important. Long ago the Tantrics expressed similar ideas. The final goal of the sex ritual is mutual pleasure and cosmic consciousness.

There are changes in the phases of the female sexual response cycle, just as in the male, but these should not cause any woman to be sexually handicapped.

The first sign of sexual excitement in the female, vaginal lubrication, is produced more slowly, and to a lesser degree. Younger women take fifteen to thirty seconds to get wet, while it may take four or five minutes of stimulation for older women to reach readiness for penetration. The clitoris may get smaller, but it continues to respond to stimulation and to transmit sexual excitement.

By allowing a little more time for nature to take her course, couples may learn to cherish and enjoy the longer period of foreplay and stimulation. Remember, pleasure comes from all over the body, not just the genitals.

Older women, like older men, usually experience a shorter orgasmic phase. As she gets older, a woman may have only four or five vaginal contractions rather than eight or twelve. Only one or two uterine contractions may be identifiable instead of three to five. The resolution phase is more rapid.

Hormone research from Masters and Johnson confirms the experience of Tantric yoginis. Sexually active women overcome the effects of estrogen starvation on the sexual parts by having intercourse frequently. If this pleasant and mutually cooperative method of keeping up one's health is not available there is always self-stimulation. Estrogen therapy in pills and injections is also possible, if medically indicated, although it is controversial.

Through the breathing exercises and proper meditation, as mentioned earlier, most people can learn to avoid or cure hypertension, some kinds of ulcers, migraine headaches. They can warm their hands by learning to concentrate on warm hands, which results in an increased flow of blood. This same mechanism can be used to bring an increased blood supply to the penis, causing erection, or to the vagina, to bring on lubrication. The possibilities in this direction are still unexplored.

The mechanism that makes possible Tantra's claims for a potent old age works in a number of ways. First of all, the tremendously positive attitude toward sex, with no idea of sexual sin, allows us to overcome the interference of guilt. Guilt about sex is rampant in our culture, whether it has been taught to us outright or absorbed indirectly.

Besides shutting out the spectre of guilt in his long black habit, the practice of meditation, of keeping the mind focused on one point, allows us to keep out all other inhibitions. These may be memories of past failures, even traumatic sexual experiences, everyday problems, or simply someone making noise in the next room. We learn how to concentrate on the vital burning flame of desire and the erotic stimuli.

Next, we know from the practice of deep breathing and mind control that no matter what the circumstances, no matter how rushed and pressured our lives, we can relax both our bodies and our minds at will.

A Tantric world view helps solve the problem of aesthetics in our youth-oriented culture. Age is considered attractive and is highly respected by Tantrics. An unlined, fatty young face with no character or experience etched in is simply not preferred to the noble face of a Tantric yogi or yogini over sixty, with luminous eyes radiating joy, self-command and understanding. Their bodies will be slim, firm, graceful and supple from years of yoga. Their air of serenity and compassion in the midst of worldly turmoil and insecurity will be attractive to both sexes. They will have avoided plagues such as ulcers, hypertension and heart trouble.

Unlike most middle-aged American males, a Tantric's powers of psychic arousal will not have been extinguished. If anything, sexual arousal will have become a conditioned response to either mental or tactile stimuli. Since sex has never been a form of conquest or domination, nor a performance in which one shoots for records to prop a shaky ego, the slight changes that occur with age will not be damaging to a Tantric's sex life.

And these changes will be far less for people who have kept up an active sex life. Use and stimulation keep the blood supply flowing, to nourish the sex organs so that degeneration of the tissues is far less than in someone who has neglected this vital function.

For the fortunate ones who succeed in awakening the often unused inner energy, Kundalini, which sleeps in us all, mental vitality will not decrease. André Gide showed an intuitive knowledge of Kundalini when he wrote, "There was a time when I was cruelly tormented, indeed obsessed by desire, and I prayed, 'Oh, let the moment come when my subjugated flesh will allow me to give myself entirely to . . .' But to what? To art? To pure thought? To God? How ignorant I was! How mad. It was the same as believing that the flame would burn brighter in a lamp with no oil left. If it were abstract my thought would go out; even today it is my carnal self that feeds the flame, and now I pray that I may retain carnal desire until I die."*

Many people may be surprised to learn that a man over fifty can be a better lover because of changes in the second, or plateau, stage of the sexual cycle. He will feel less driven to come and can stay hard for a long time after reaching a completely pleasurable level of sexual tension.

Besides getting used to these small changes, the man may need to restructure his value system when he retires. He may want to concentrate on conserving and enjoying rather than achieving and acquiring; on concern for others rather than control of others; on being rather than doing. Freed from the pressures to prove himself a super-competent success, the mature lover may find more time and a healthier attitude for savoring all that life still has to offer—including sex and the study of Tantra.

Goethe wrote of experiencing a second puberty during his later years. Actually there may be several during a life. This is not only a sudden upsurge of sexual desires, but also a repetition of the stirring ecstasies which accompanied the first puberty. Like the first, the second puberty can lead to an enormous expansion of understanding and awareness, creating fresh energies and inspirations. Just as the desire of the first puberty is often not expressed directly but idealized in hero worship or love from afar, the same can be true of the last. But if he wants it, the older man can usually find a flesh and blood Shakti for direct expression of his sexual yearning.

Older women meet far more social difficulties. Love is hard to find, even to buy, especially if a woman has not made herself

* Beauvoir, Simone de. *The Coming of Age.* New York; G. P. Putnam's Sons, 1972, p. 351.

interesting and charming. The problem of finding and keeping a man's love becomes more difficult the more passive she has been. One of the few rays of hope for a full life for aging women, until the recent work by Masters and Johnson, came from the letters of Colette. Over the years she wrote to her best friend expressing her wonder not only at finding sexual desire in herself, but also at her good fortune in finding a young man to love her in her old age.

If they are alone, women, and men too, might follow the example of Tibetan nuns and harness their fantasies to keep the erotic furnace fueled. This can be done by choosing a Yidam. I'll introduce you to your Yidam in Chapter 13.

12 *Erotic Exercises*

AMERICAN WOMEN, and most women all over the world, neglect the two muscles in their bodies that are the most important for sexual pleasure. Our adolescent sexuality is so focused on our breasts that many women do some sort of exercises for their pectoral muscles, but most are unaware that they even have a levator vaginae or a constrictor cunni. The former encircles the vagina and the latter, the entrance. Unless a woman has never had children, she is likely to have (as I did after the birth of two nine-pound babies), a loose, scarred and stretched vagina. This can be remedied by exercises or, if need be, surgery. A friend of mine, one of two who had surgery in India to tighten the vagina simply to increase pleasure for themselves and their husbands, recently told me that an American gynecologist who detected the surgery asked her who had talked her into wasting her money. This is one small indication of the sexual negativism of many members of the American medical profession.

HAREM EXERCISES FOR HOUSEWIVES In most cases the following exercises, if practiced methodically, will do away with the need for surgery (as they did in my case) and restore a virginal tightness to the vagina, as well as giving the control of the most accomplished harem favorite—called a *Kabbayah*, or holder.

Both the levator vaginae and the constrictor cunni are volun-

148

tary, striated muscles, which means that they can be taught to respond at will. The idea is to learn to squeeze and grasp and suck with the vagina. Try inserting the first two fingers into the vagina to see if you can feel any muscle action at all as you attempt this. Push down hard, as if defecating, then pull in as hard as you can, as if trying to stop urination and defecation. Keep trying ten or twelve times until you begin to feel some action. With time and concentration, the ability to contract these muscles can be developed and improved. Of course, practice this during intercourse. This is best done in the lateral or side position or with the man on top. Men should all learn to remain motionless a few seconds after entering the vagina in order to allow it to contract and adjust to the size of the phallus.

Later on, learn to squeeze one finger with the vaginal muscles. Try to use the two sets of muscles separately if possible, but don't worry about it if you find that you can't. This is a very fine point of expertise. Once you are familiar with them, you can practice the exercises at will without the need of a finger or penis. This is an excellent way to keep your sexuality alive during famine periods (such as business trips) when there is no man in your life. It is far more sound, I believe, than using a vibrator, which may spoil a woman and does not prepare her as well as the exercises do to share pleasure with a man. By using these muscles, a woman can bring the man to orgasm while enjoying the most intense orgasms of her life without the need for thrashing and ball-bearing action of the hips and pelvis. After he has come she can wait a few seconds, then use the constricting (but not the pushing) movements, which all men (except those who are hypersensitive after orgasm) find delightful. If he is unusually vigorous, this may reawaken him before he knows what is happening, for he may never have felt this before. No wonder harem girls were taught to pick up rounded pencil-like objects with their vaginas!

Don't worry if at first you find your neglected vagina to be totally unresponsive and loose. The penis is singularly undemanding and easy to please and will be happy even in a slack enclosure.

There are two additional methods that can be used to increase pleasure in the female. Masters and Johnson report that many women tighten the buttocks to augment tension and feeling, which is similar to the way to Tantrics awaken Kundalini by tightening the anal sphincter. Bonnie Prudden suggests moving the pelvis backward in most sexual positions to intensify friction on the clitoris.

For variety there are a number of useful pelvic exercises that can be learned at home by yourself. Remember to combine all these exercises with deep, relaxed breathing.

Practice the corkscrew motion that is so enjoyable when the woman is on top. Get down on all fours and imagine that you are burrowing into a cork, or let your fantasy be explicit. In any case, move your hips in a circular motion, tracing a circle several times clockwise, then counterclockwise. This is marvelous for both the back and stomach, and for pleasure.

Practice moving the pelvis back and forth while standing and again on all fours. Stick your tail out like a duck, then pull it under as hard as you can several times. Arch your back like a cat and then let it sway like a pitiful horse. You too can bump and grind like an erotic dancer, all the while loosening your orgasm reflex.

Then stand again and sway your hips from side to side like a golfer.

Again down on all fours and wag your tail.

Then put all these exercises together and move.

13 Sleep with Your Head in the Lap of Your Yidam—Fantasies

THIS, DEAR READER, is more your chapter than mine, for your Yidam belongs to you alone.

In Tibetan Tantra a disciple chooses a special Yidam, or Tara, when female, to be his protector and prays to him or her every night. These are deities representing psychological truths such as fear, anger and, most often, compassion. Among Tantrics in Nepal and Tibet, the idea of Yidams is so much a part of life that artists paint pictures of them, authors describe them, and sculptors make tactile Yidams of gilded bronze. Many believers "see" their Yidams through visualization, by carrying the common practice of fantasy to unique levels. Your Yidam or Tara can remain eternally at your side. In Tibetan monasteries each monk believes his own Tara sleeps on his pillow and cushions his head, after making a canopy of crossed scepters to cover the bed.

When he represents compassion, the Yidam has a serene Buddha image; but sometimes he is chosen to represent the disciple's worst faults. There is a whole realm of malevolent gods in fierce (Heruka) form to choose from to help you deal with your antisocial tendencies. He may represent your greatest human failing, such as stupidity, anger, envy, or cruelty, and help you to master it.

Beautiful Tibetan Yidams are described in the following terms. "Their upper garments are of divine silken stuff ornamented with bold designs in gold. Soft of hand, supple of body and limbs, sleek of skin, sinuously waisted, youthful, shining, pure of form, they possess countless sorts of excellence and splendour."* But you may choose anyone to be your Yidam or Tara, anyone you have ever loved. You may speak to the Yidam in the Tibetan manner—"Ha, Diamond Being, how radiant is the state we share, bound with the iron chain of sympathetic joy!"—or in the current slang. Your Yidam will always love you.

Often the Yidam and his Tara are shown united in Yab-Yum to make the concept of oneness more real. But since my Yidam is my fantasy and mine alone, I banish this consort and keep my Yidam all to myself, indulging my possessive urges where they do no harm.

Your Yidam (or Tara) can help you with your sexual development as well as your spiritual liberation. If, even after reading this far, you still can't accept an active role in sex, imagine your Yidam taking you forcefully for his consort, leading you through the sexual asanas. He can help tear you out of yourself if you still can't let go.

Your fantasy can initiate you into the Tantric secret ceremonies. He or she can give you the ability to be alone by providing mystical contact and inspiration. One advantage of choosing a Tibetan Yidam for your fantasy is that he may have as many as twelve arms and hands to use to do lovely things to you—anything at all you want. Two of his hands can hold your buttocks, as is shown occasionally in the Yab-Yum icons, while other hands cup your face, hold your breasts, and touch your private places. He always looks into the eyes of his Shakti (you) without shame, fear or disgust at your sexiness.

Having a Yidam can allow you to try every act you ever dreamed of, even if your mate doesn't approve, and still remain monogamous.

If there is the touch of the voyeur in you, and yet you could never make the group sex scene or 42nd Street in New York City, watch your Yidam and his consort do everything conceivable.

If you are in the mood to be an exhibitionist, have the consort watch everything between you and your Yidam.

Since it is your fantasy, there is no reason to limit yourself to acts with one Yidam. Have a plurality of partners if you like. There are countless celestial beings, so you may conjure up Dakinis, Devas, etc. Make them all happy.

If you want to be licked all over, your guardian angel will be glad to please.

* Blofeld, John. *The Way of Power: A Practical Guide to the Tantric Mysticism of Tibet.* Ruskin House, 1970, p. 208.

Visualization allows you to prolong your rapture whether you're alone or with a partner. The power of fantasy can aid in control of your erection or moist female expectation, and finally in mind-blowing orgasm.

See your Yidam as a seventeen-year-old boy, or fantasize Tara's cosmic yoni. Relive your first great sexual experience, detail by detail.

No matter what the circumstances, even in solitary confinement, your spirit, and therefore your body, need never be lonely and neglected. Visualize to arouse and stimulate neglected nerves in your body. Feed the erect growth with your thoughts, memories and dreams; irrigate the throbbing yoni with your own sweet blood. Nourish your nervous system and responses.

Arouse the serpent current by constricting the anus. Continue meditation right to the explosion of the lifted jet and muscular convulsions that come with the lightning of that union in your head. Celebrate a spurting fountain of white bindu in offering to Tara. KRI-I-IM.*

If, unfortunately, you are a man whose penis seems more like a murderous weapon wanting to pierce than an instrument of pleasure, then by all means, please use it on your Tara. If, regrettably, you want to flagellate, humiliate, or urinate on your sex partner, please do it to your Tara. Save acts worthy of the Marquis de Sade for your private fantasies and not for little girls. This is what the Yidam and Tara are for.

Don't kill your life urges. Practice using your sex force in a positive way with your Yidam, for energy, liberation and growth.

---

* A common mantra.

14 *Decorating the Bedroom to Inspire Lust (The Goddess Rati)*

AMERICANS SPEND more money on their kitchens and baths than on any other rooms of the house. My Indian friends spent more money on their bedrooms, the temples of pleasure. I stayed in the palaces of a half-dozen maharajas in India and never saw a kitchen. The bathrooms were adequate and had a simple cup on the floor next to the toilet or on the sink, used for washing the private parts, like a bidet. The bedrooms, however, were magnificent. This may say something about comparative values.

Two of the most sensuously decorated bedrooms were in the Lake Palace in Udaipur, now a hotel. In the bridal suite, the walls were covered with paintings of beautiful girls with swelling figures and tiny blouses that covered only the tops of their breasts, long skirts, and transparent veils on their heads in the Rajasthani fashion. A heavy gold-framed mirror was set into the ceiling to reflect the hopefully amorous activity of the night or day.

The other bedroom looked out over the lake from windows set with colored glass. The jewel colors were reflected on the bed, on the floor, on the ceiling, everywhere. A swing, large enough for two, hung from the ceiling on chains made of brass figures of animals and birds.

The palace gave me ideas and suggestions for decorating erotically. If a brazen mirror over the bed is too obvious for your own taste, or your mother-in-law's, the mirror can be placed on a door that can be opened at the proper angle, or hung low over a dressing table. Use of a mirror appeals to the element of the voyeur in most of us and stimulates our narcissism. Seeing yourself making love is fantastically exciting. A mirror is especially useful during foreplay. You can star in your own erotic film.

Have a subtle light in the bedroom. Most civilized lovers and all Tantrics consider it barbaric to make love in the dark. In the dark you would miss the look of ecstasy and peace that comes over both faces after orgasm. You would miss the sight of the partner's body with the nipples standing and the miraculous rise of the penis, which is particularly exciting if the man has not been circumsized so that the dark pink tip appears when stimulated. The light can be so dim that wrinkles disappear and both lovers are made more lovely by the soft light.

Another addition to the bedroom, to bring all the senses into play, is an incense burner. Burning incense during love-making increases enjoyment by adding an element that can range from the exotic to the reverent, depending on the scent chosen and its associations.

Many people find a water bed exciting because it does seem to add to the feeling of being part of the cosmic ocean.

The rich, luxurious touches found in palaces and eighteenth-century boudoirs, such as elegant furniture, gilt-framed works of art, velvets, furs and satins, may appeal to most tastes. On the other hand, a friend tells me she was most touched by a writer's ascetic cell and monk's bed. I can see how such utter simplicity would inspire a woman to give the velvet of her own skin, the copper, gold, or onyx of her hair, her secret jewels hidden in fur.

So there is no set rule for inviting Rati, the lovely goddess of lust, to steal into your bed. She brought life and joy to Kama, her consort, in the simplicity of a bed of leaves in the forest. Nothing will keep her out of yours if you want her.

Conclusion

IN SHORT, fellow seekers, holy Yab-Yum is yum yum. Keep the jewel in the lotus whenever you can.

OM
MANI
PADME
HUM

Glossary of Tantric Terms

Kama	God of love.
Kundalini	A form of mystic life-force, coiled like a sleeping serpent near the base of the spine; called the Serpent Power. She can be aroused by yogic discipline, especially sexual, sometimes by meditation.
Lingam	The penis, symbol of the god Shiva.
Maithuna	Sexual intercourse, usually in a ritual context.
Prana	Cosmic energy.
Shakti	The divine consort of the god Shiva, or the ritual sex partner of the Tantric.
Shastra	Teachings or scriptures.
Yab-Yum	Sexual union; literally, "mother-father."
Yoni	The female genitals.
Yogi	Follower of yoga. Feminine form: *yogini*.
Nirvana	Liberation; supreme bliss, cosmic consciousness, samadhi.
Moksha	Nirvana, in Sanskrit.
Mantra	Verbal formula to call up conditioned response.
Muladhara chakra	One of the six nerve centers of importance in the body. This symbolic center is located between the anus and the genitals.

Selected Reading List

Avalon, Arthur (Sir John Woodroffe). *Principles of Tantra*. London; Luzac & Co., 1916.
———. *The Great Liberation, Mahanirvana Tantra*. Madras; Ganesh and Co., 1927.
Barber, Theodore, ed. *Biofeedback and Self Control*. Chicago & N.Y.; Aldine, 1971.
Beauvoir, Simone de. *The Coming of Age*. N.Y.; G. P. Putnam's Sons, 1972.
Berry, Gerald. *Religions of the World*. N.Y.; Barnes and Noble, 1947.
Blofeld, John. *The Way of Power: A Practical Guide to the Tantric Mysticism of Tibet*. Ruskin House, 1970.
Burton, Sir Richard, trans. *The Ananga Ranga of Kalyana Malla*. Kama Shastra Society of London, 1885; Library of Congress.
Burton, Sir Richard, trans. *The Kama Sutra of Vatsyayana*. New Delhi, 1960, and N.Y.; Capricorn Books, 1963.
Chakra Magazine. Kumar Gallery, New Delhi, India.
Chakravarti, Chintaharan. *Tantras*. Calcutta; Punth Pustak, 1963.
Chang, Garma. *Teachings of Tibetan Yoga*. N.Y.; University Books, 1963.
Elisofon, Eliot, and Alan Watts. *Erotic Spirituality: The Vision of Konarak*. N.Y.; The Macmillan Co., 1971.
Garrison, Omar V. *Tantra: The Yoga of Sex*. N.Y.; Vulcan Press, 1964.
Havell, E. B. *The Art Heritage of India*. Bombay; Taraporevala, 1956.
Inkeles, Gordon, and Murray Todris. *The Art of Sensual Massage*. San Francisco; Straight Arrow Books, 1972.
Krishna, Gopi. *Kundalini*. Berkeley; Shambala Press, 1971.
Marqués-Rivière, Jean. *Tantrik Yoga: Hindu and Tibetan*. London; Rider and Co., 1940.
Mookerjee, Ajit. *Tantra Art: Its Philosophy and Physics*. Basel, Switzerland; Ravi Kumar, 1966.
Randhawa, M. S. *Kangra Paintings of the Bhagavata Purana*. New Delhi; National Museum, 1963.

————. *Kangra Paintings of the Gita Govinda*. New Delhi; National Museum, 1963.
Rawson, Philip. *Erotic Art of the East*. N.Y.; Minerva, 1968.
————. *Tantra: The Indian Cult of Ecstasy*. London; Avon, 1973.
————. *The Art of Tantra*. New York Graphic Society, 1973.
————. Selected Writings. N.Y.; Farrar, Straus & Giroux, 1970.
Reich. Wilhelm. The Sexual Revolution. N.Y.; Orgone Inst. Press, 1945.
Scott, G. R. *Far Eastern Sex Life*. London; Gerald Swan, 1949.
Thomas, P. *Kama Kalpa, or the Hindu Ritual of Love*. Bombay; Taraporevala Sons, 1956.
Watts, Alan. *Nature, Man and Woman*. N.Y.; Vintage Books, 1958.
Woodroffe, Sir John (Arthur Avalon). *Mahamaya: The World as Power*. Madras; Ganesh and Co., 1929, 1966.
————. *Shakti and Shakta*. Madras; Ganesh and Co., 3rd ed., 1929.